Appreciative Inquiry

as a

Daily Leadership

Practice

FOREWORD BY RONALD FRY

LUC VERHEIJEN
SASKIA TJEPKEMA
JOERI KABALT

Appreciative Inquiry as a Daily Leadership Practice

Cover photo by Sanne Kabalt
First translation by Russell Kerkhoven
Edited by Ronald Fry
Cover and interior design by Debbi Stocco

Taos Institute Publications
A Division of the Taos Institute
Chagrin Falls, Ohio
USA

ISBN-13: 978-1-938552-75-5

Library of Congress Control Number: 2020930881

Introduction to
Taos Institute Publications

The Taos Institute is a nonprofit organization dedicated to the development of social constructionist theory and practice for purposes of world benefit. Constructionist theory and practice locate the source of meaning, value, and action in communicative relations among people. Our major investment is in fostering relational processes that can enhance the welfare of people and the world in which they live. Taos Institute Publications offers contributions to cutting-edge theory and practice in social construction. Our books are designed for scholars, practitioners, students, and the openly curious public. The **Children's Books Series** is our newest series of books related to social construction and positive change in the world. The **Focus Book Series** provides brief introductions and overviews that illuminate theories, concepts, and useful practices. The **Tempo Book Series** is especially dedicated to the general public and to practitioners. The **Books for Professionals Series** provides in-depth works that focus on recent developments in theory and practice. **WorldShare Books** is an online offering of books in PDF format for free download from our website. Our books are particularly relevant to social scientists and to practitioners concerned with individual, family, organizational, community, and societal change.

— Kenneth J. Gergen
President, Board of Directors
The Taos Institute

Taos Institute Board of Directors

Harlene Anderson	Mary Gergen	Monica Sesma
Duane Bidwell	Kenneth J. Gergen	Sally St. George
Celiane Camargo Borges	Sheila McNamee	Dan Wulff

David Cooperrider, Emeritus   Diana Whitney, Emerita

WorldShare Books Senior Editors:
Kenneth Gergen, Dan Wulff and Mary Gergen

Books for Professional Series Editor
Kenneth Gergen

Tempo Series Editor
Mary Gergen

Focus Book Series Editor
Harlene Anderson

Executive Director
Dawn Dole

For information about the Taos Institute and social constructionism visit:
www.taosinstitute.net

CONTENTS

FOREWORD

By *Ronald Fry*, Case Western Reserve University, Cleveland, Ohio, USA

The literature on Appreciative Inquiry (AI) has grown consistently and dramatically over the past three decades since being introduced. From thick and thin primers on the foundational principles and the "4 (or 5!) D" intervention model to contextual applications (coaching, churches, six-sigma, program evaluation, outdoor education, peace initiatives, healthcare, communities, education, military, and numerous corporate case studies), this body of applied scholarship has broadened and deepened our understanding of how strength-based, positive change can enable flourishing at the individual, group, and larger system levels. In this contribution to the AI literature, authors Luc Verheijen, Saskia Tjepkema, and Joeri Kabalt add significantly to this trajectory. Specifically they deepen our awareness of how to "be" in appreciative inquiry (not just "do," "apply," or "follow" it) and they broaden our perspectives on how to adapt, flex, or even play with the foundational ideas, beyond the now "traditional" discovery-dream-design-destiny flow of activity.

There is much to glean from this work, whether you are a practiced expert in AI or a novice, a facilitator or a manager, or reading from personal or professional curiosity. I am grateful to the authors for the opportunity to share (in no particular order) a few of the things that stand out most to me; my personal view of some "gems" embedded in these pages.

Shift in Focus from Positivity to Generativity

I appreciate the authors' strong assertion that, in their experiences with AI, it has become more and more apparent that the intention or purpose of applying AI principles is *not* to make people feel better; to experience more positive emotions. Rather, the focus on positivity (positive images attract positive action) is a means to an end – a necessary ingredient for generative connections that ignite sustainable collaboration. A generative connection is a unique emergence of ideation in a space where those coming up with new ideas *also* connect in a way that makes them want to work on those ideas further. They self-organize and "own" taking initiative instead of waiting to be given permission or to be delegated a follow-up task. Several of the authors' stories reveal this remarkable potential with AI where stakeholders, who otherwise would not be asking for more work or added responsibility, in fact, come out of an "AI experience" having volunteered to take on more responsibility and do more work to achieve a shared desired future outcome. In my humble opinion, it is paramount for the worldwide community of AI practice to understand this distinction. The amazing force of positivity, supported now by nearly two decades of scientific research,[1] is in service of an experiential outcome where generative collaboration emerges through self-managed, multi-stakeholder groupings. The work with AI is therefore not about positivity as much as it is about fostering generative collaborations.

The Generative Power of Stories

Staying with the theme of generativity, the numerous examples shared in this work all point to the generative power of story-seeking, story-telling, and story-listening. The authors model this in the way they weave all kinds of stories throughout the text. I love the richness of many of the stories in this book that expose more of the inner experience of managers and leaders while and after they engaged with AI. Each account paints a new canvas for the reader to imagine additional possibilities; *not* a best solution or expert advice on how AI should be conducted. Narratives have always been deeply rooted in AI practice[2] and with the advent of neuroscience we are beginning to learn more about why sharing good stories might enhance cooperation, trigger compassion, and foster a helping orientation through the release of the hormone Oxytocin when we listen to a good story.[3]

Generative Space

I have often thought of working with AI as if choreographing collaborative spaces. While my focus has been mainly on the interactive nature of that "space" the authors here go further and deeper into the design of spaces for human systems to flourish within. They look at the meaning of space from a relational, physical and aesthetic perspective. They describe often how they improvise in the moment to create special cues and emotional reactions to accompany the task or issue being discussed or explored. This mindful attention to a holistic construct of "space" is a unique gift from this book.

Emergence over Form

As the authors blend case examples and stories with interpretive concepts, they weave a tapestry for us that sends another important message, perhaps "between the lines." They do state that working with AI cannot and should not be formulaic, as if putting people through fixed steps or a rigid sequence of conversations. But the way they go back and forth between planning and designing prior to an AI intervention, and then flexing and improvising during said intervention communicates an even deeper message. To be truly in a stance of inquiry – and never forget AI is about a type of inquiry – we must be open to emergence, open to new ideas, meanings, perspectives we did not have prior. Even the classic AI Cycle of Definition, Discovery, Dream, Design and Destiny, while logically based on the foundational principles, can easily be experienced as a forced march toward predictive outcomes. In fact, as the authors' examples boldly imply, the conversations in each of these so-called phases *should* lead to unpredicted, surprising, or even unsettling outcomes. Otherwise we are not learning from the inquiry at hand. Through this message about valuing emergence, this is the first book (to my knowledge) that connects the practice of AI with the ideas of organizing as Complex Responsive Processes. Influenced by the works of Ralph Stacey and his notions of complexity,[4] this perspective of so-called human systems boils down to this; the root of all organizing lies in conversations, each with its own unique flow of gestures and responses. One may begin with a gesture (assertion or question) that has intention or even predictability behind it, but once the response is given, the parties in the conversation are now in uncharted waters. Shared meanings, differences, conflicts, agreements, etc. *emerge* from this complex and uncontrollable interplay of gesture and response. This aligns strongly with the social constructionist principles underlying AI from its inception; words create worlds, questions are fateful, and to change something, begin by changing the way you are conversing about it.

This may be the most important contribution from this book – a bold calling (not just a reminder) that in order to "be" or to embody AI, we must also be truly open to emergence. That means to expect it in our planning and design of AI activities, and to flex with it or lean into it once we are in those generative spaces. This is important for both the AI practitioner and the participants, or co-inquirers. Appreciative Inquiry is about inquiring into something we desire from a lens that values strengths and positive anticipatory images. In that inquiry, we appreciate or value sincerely all that emerges. This book is full of suggestions, examples, and ideas about how to be in this frame of mind and action. By underscoring and appreciating the power of emergence, the authors draw our attention to the idea of *anticipatory learning* that can (only) come from generative connections – the real promise of AI.

[1] cf Fredrickson, B. (2009) *Positivity: Ground-Breaking Research Reveals How to Embrace the Hidden Strength of Positive Emotions, Overcome Negativity and Thrive*. Random House: New York
[2] Barrett, F & R. Fry (2005) *Appreciative Inquiry: A Positive approach to Building Cooperative Capacity*. Taos Publications: Chagrin Falls, OD.
[3] Zach, P. J. (2015) "Why Inspiring Stories Make Us React: The Neuroscience of Narrative." *Cerebrum*, Jan-Feb: 2
[4] Stacey, R. (2001) *Complex Responsive Processes in Organizations*. Routledge: London

INTRODUCTION:
BACKGROUND AND STRUCTURE OF THIS BOOK

"The future is not some place we are going to, but one we are creating. The paths are not to be found, but made, and the activity of making them, changes both the maker and the destination."
– John Schaar (1928-2011)

As a leader, there is always something new you want to achieve with your organization and team. It may be a new way of working, improved collaboration with another department, a change of focus for the whole organization, a fresh approach to external collaboration, a more innovative culture, or…

How do you approach your goal in such a way that it leads to sustainable change? How do you ensure that the process itself is energizing for you and all the other people involved? And how can you access and make use of all of the knowledge and experience of your organization or team, and create co-ownership of the change?

Organization and team development have increasingly become everyday components of a leader's role. Sometimes, they concern organization-wide changes with a distinct beginning and end – a program-like change in which you are called upon to take an active role, as being responsible for the implementation or as a pioneer. Even more interesting are those developments that emerge from your own vision and drive: improvements that don't translate into a dedicated, explicit change program, but that you seek to implement in and on the job, in everyday practice.

This book is aimed at informal and formal leaders who aspire to get things done; to realize meaningful changes in everyday practices that will lead to a better performance and at the same time contribute to a vitalizing and energizing working environment. These types of change processes often cannot be planned or controlled in detail, but they can be initiated with intent and be supported and encouraged from your position as a leader.

APPRECIATIVE INQUIRY

Appreciative Inquiry (AI) is an approach to change that has increasingly gained ground. Developed in the USA, the practice of AI with its worldwide recognition as a refreshing theory and method of change, has also grown more and more in Europe in the past decade. It is a perspective, a way of looking or even a way of *being* in your job that focuses on what gives life, on opportunities and on generative energy. It is an approach that is more developmental than strictly change-oriented. It draws on capacities and strengths. Rather than implementing, it focuses on continuously inquiring, experimenting and playing around with new ideas. It sees organizing and changing as relational processes: *doing together* through powerful collaborative relations, active engagement and by entering into continuous dialogue – internally and externally. This vision and approach enables leaders to bring about smaller or larger changes *with* the involvement of employees, clients, and other stakeholders.

An essential starting point of Appreciative Inquiry is that change happens one conversation at a time. The big change happens in the small moment. And the small moments become the bigger movement. This provides opportunities and leads one to view every day and even every encounter as an opportunity for the desired development to come into being. It presupposes a specific way of looking at leadership and change with an accompanying repertoire that includes leading by asking questions, encouraging and supporting exactly those initiatives where change is beginning to happen, and catalyzing the energy and ideas that are already present amongst employees.

We are very enthusiastic about Appreciative Inquiry, both as change theory, and as a daily management practice. We observe and note that in many instances this way of working enables people to develop exceptional and surprising innovations, in a way that fuels pride and job satisfaction, while strengthening mutual connectivity, leading to more effective and healthier work places.

THIS BOOK

This book is titled *Appreciative Inquiry as a daily leadership practice*. It offers lessons from the field to help expand manager's capacities to bring out the best in people while organizing for a common good. Our purpose is to inspire leaders, whether formal or informal, to develop their daily practices from an Appreciative Inquiry perspective. To live the underlying principles and to realize that change happens one conversation at a time. The book intends to support you as a companion on your route to applying Appreciative Inquiry in your own way.

By combining a theoretical perspective with an abundance of examples and practical ideas and guidelines, we hope to provide a helpful instrument and source of inspiration and understanding. We added personal vignettes: portraits of leaders who consciously or unconsciously apply and live Appreciative Inquiry principles or methods. We offer examples of intentional change interventions that increase levels of energy and inspiration – for example: articulating an affirmative topic for the intended change, organizing round table sessions during which staff members can exchange success stories, or creating change through designing a cycle of experiments. We also reflect on what you can do in your daily work practice in conversations with fellow workers – think of performance reviews, team meetings and casual conversations that happen near the coffee machine.

We draw upon published literature and research in the field, on our own experience as consultants, coaches and interim-managers, on stories and experiences of people we've worked with and conferences that we've attended and co-organized with fellow professionals. In the past years, we followed a steep learning curve on Appreciative Inquiry and Appreciative Leadership; through applying, talking, thinking and reading about it, and now through writing about it. This book was published in Dutch by Boom Publishers, Amsterdam, in the spring of 2016. To our wonder and with gratitude, the book has found its way to many readers in our region and has been reprinted several times since its initial publication. Encouragement from good friends and colleagues has led to the translation and this publication of the English version by Taos Institute Publications.

AN OVERVIEW OF THE BOOK

This book contains five sections. In every section you will find several short chapters. These can be read in any order and each contains a distinct perspective on the theme. You can browse through the book and just read the chapters that catch your eye, or if you would prefer to read the book from cover-to-cover, that is most certainly possible as well. Our key point is: the book is not a step-by-step guide. Rather it is a collection of ideas and examples of AI in practice that we hope will help any reader to begin to experiment, inquire, and develop as an Appreciative Leader.

In the first section, we outline our perspective on Appreciative Inquiry and its foundations. What is it? Where does it come from? What makes it relevant? And which perspectives on leadership and change is it rooted in? This first section (by far the longest) has a different, more reflective and theoretical character than the other sections, and as such it lays the groundwork for what follows. If you would like to understand our viewpoints on Appreciative Inquiry, and/or if you are new to AI, it might be useful to read this first.

In section two we focus on the underlying principles and most significant mechanisms of Appreciative Inquiry. How do you come to an appealing direction or image as the starting point for a change? How do you orchestrate change in such a way that it gives space for others to contribute? Who do you include as fellow inquirer or designer of the change process? How can you deal effectively with so called negative emotions such as resistance and fear?

The third section zooms in on the good conversation as one of the most important ingredients of Appreciative Inquiry. Conversational practices are at the heart of AI. How do you create conversations during which new ideas surface and energy for action emerges? How do you recognize them? As a leader how do you encourage these conversations? How can you use the strength of generative questions and stories? How can you lead the process from talk to action?

The fourth section has a more practical focus. What concrete forms or methods could you use to apply Appreciative Inquiry? How do you encourage people to enter into conversations on what works well and what provides energy in your team or organization? How do you use the past as a stepping stone for transformation? How do you collectively envision the desired future or change direction? How can you entice people to make a start with their own experiments in their work setting?

In the fifth section we address what is specifically required of you as a leader or facilitator of change. How can you honestly realize the true potential of people and groups you work with? How can you encourage people to progress in small steps? How do you give enough space to others, while you continue to aim for the bigger change that you envision as a leader? How do you focus your attention?

We conclude the book with an epilogue, written by Dr. Rene Bouwen, emeritus professor at the Catholic University Leuven and a pioneer of Appreciative Inquiry. He puts the appreciating-inquiring approach in a broader frame of social learning and organizing processes.

We hope you enjoy the book and that you will find new and inspirational ideas for your own leadership practice.

By Luc Verheijen, Saskia Tjepkema and Joeri Kabalt,
Fall 2015 (Dutch manuscript), Fall 2019 (English manuscript)

INTERVIEW: HERMAN NIJNS - RANDSTAD BELGIUM

"TO ME IT IS ABOUT THE ANECDOTES AND STORIES BEHIND THE NUMBERS - PEOPLE'S LIVES."

Herman Nijns is CEO of Randstad Belgium, a large and well-known temping agency. He worked his way up the entire corporate ladder before assuming the top executive role in 2005. In Belgium, Randstad is a pioneer in the application of Appreciative Inquiry. The AI philosophy fits the culture of the organization and the values of this chief executive like a glove.

AI FITS OUR WAY OF WORKING

As far as I know, Randstad was one of the first organizations to adopt an AI approach in Belgium: this was around 1997. Back then, we were in the midst of formulating a long-term vision for the company answering the question, what are the strengths of our past and how do we look toward the future? As senior management team we were looking for concepts that could work for us, and we met with leadership consultant Herman Wittockx, who suggested working with Appreciative Inquiry. We immediately felt that this philosophy was a good fit. Randstad has a culture of cooperation and we always seek to mobilize the strengths of our people. AI fit our identity and strengthened it at the same time.

CHOOSING YOUR FOCUS

For me, the essence of AI is a deliberate choice to focus on what is going well, to discover the qualities that can serve as building blocks for the next steps. To work from your own strengths and personal experiences. I find that such a focus always promotes growth at organizational as well as product levels. The exercise that I engaged in with my management team to develop a long-term vision for Randstad Belgium is perhaps the best illustration. I recall an event that happened shortly after I had been appointed as General Director. I was very keen to share with my colleagues my vision for the future; in my mind, Randstad could evolve from a temporary employment agency to an organization that assists people at crossroads in their professional career paths. How could I share this dream in an inspirational manner? I told a story, based on one of my family pictures. By sharing the life stories of the people in the picture, I illustrated how Randstad could help people in the job market, and the importance of providing that support.

FROM INDIVIDUAL DREAM TO SHARED INSPIRATION

For me, that example contains a second core element of AI: always trying to move from individual dream to shared inspiration. For that, you need a dream to begin with, so that others can recognize where you want to go, and you can invite them to join and expand the dream. In my case, our management team stepped in and together we elaborated on the inspiration and images in a strategic five-year plan, business models and measurable achievements. All the time, the dream was there, working as a North Star for our progress.

WHAT (AND WHOM) ARE WE WORKING FOR?

Working with AI – which we often do implicitly in our company – is closely related to Randstad's and my core mission: to make a significant social contribution to companies and people in the job-market. This mission, to be of value to people in their career development, has always motivated me. And this is something that is applicable to our clients as well as our own staff. AI makes people feel seen and valued, for what they have to offer in terms of drive and knowledge and skills. It is exactly that starting point that we also use to support so many people outside. The fact that we reach a large and diverse client group with our way of working is of course energizing, but even more so are the anecdotes and stories behind the data – the people behind it. And the difference we make in their lives. This is the reason we do our job, and that is what I want to continue to hear and feel. The type of entrepreneurship that is grounded in moral choices – doing well by doing "good" – is essential for me.

WHEN THE GOING GETS TOUGH

Sometimes this requires a balancing act, especially when short term results seem to clash with the long-term vision. For instance, recently we had to make tough choices due to the need for a re-organization. At every turn in that process, I realized that we have to take a step back now, so that we can face the future with more confidence and strength. The toughest moments were when others doubted my good intentions. I want to maintain and strengthen the intrinsic value of Randstad, even if that called for a profound reorganization. I am not sure if that called for courage. In my view, courage is about daring to make a decision and face the consequences. My main aim was to offer people a perspective.

AI CAN BE A SOURCE OF INSPIRATION FOR MORE COMPANIES

Concerning the future of AI, I would hope that the discipline extends to the business environment. AI is now a strong undercurrent in our company. It is a lot stronger than the many "flavor of the month" hypes that come by. It continues to surprise me that so many companies do not recognize the power of this approach. Does that have something to do with references, discourse, with too few business cases in the various forums? Maybe Randstad could play a more prominent role in this. Or should we apply the philosophy even more explicitly in our product and service development and share our stories and experiences with other companies?

I realize that our challenge is to include the value of AI more in our organizational story as it is our way of looking to the world. I use it frequently in our team, even though I do not always call it AI. That is also my preferred way of working: when you reduce AI to a methodology, it does not work. I prefer just to do it, rather than talk about it. For example, whenever we encounter a fresh challenge, our first response is to look for examples from the past that show how we succeeded in addressing a similar issue, and what we could learn from that to improve our performance in the future. That approach helped adapt and realize our strategy and has been fruitful for Randstad. There is a foundation, a stable grounding of AI on which I can always depend. It is an approach that helps us to look towards the future with more confidence, and to continue doing so without being pulled down by the problems.

APPRECIATIVE INQUIRY: A PROCESS OF COLLECTIVE CURIOSITY

APPRECIATIVE INQUIRY: AN EXPLORATION

The core principle of Appreciative Inquiry as a change philosophy is that a system develops positively as soon as people jointly start inquiring into what works, share their expectations of the future and explore ways to realize this ideal by expanding current successes and building on strengths. In such a process, creative answers surface and new ideas come to the fore – in a way that they do not when people take a problem as their core focus and seek to analyze why something does not work. In addition, the collaborative energy level increases and a different quality of relationship develops between people whenever they jointly transform shared possibilities into action.

Appreciative Inquiry (AI) is not new. The concept emerged in the 1980s and has gradually been elaborated – both AI's practical applications as well as its theoretical underpinnings have been better grounded in the past decades. Currently, there is an increasing interest in this perspective on change and development within organizations, which seems related to current circumstances in which innovations in organizations take place. Several of the historically tried and trusted methods in the organizational development and change domain appear to have met their limitations. Organizations and their leaders want to complement their toolkit with different approaches to, and philosophies of, change. AI feeds into this, in multiple ways, as it is suited to a number of the most prevalent challenges organizations face.

In this chapter – the books most extensive – we explore AI as a theory and practice for organizational development and change. Where does AI come from? What are the underlying principles and assumptions of AI? What does a change process, shaped according to AI principles, look like? What are its implications for leadership?

AI AS A CHANGE PHILOSOPHY: ITS ORIGINS AND DEVELOPMENT

THE BEGINNING: A STUDY AT THE CLEVELAND CLINIC

In the early nineteen eighties, David Cooperrider constructed the foundations for AI, during his PhD research at Case Western Reserve University. He conducted an organizational inquiry into the culture and strategy of a large tertiary care, physician group practice: the Cleveland Clinic. He noticed that the medical staff had little time and patience for traditional feedback session of his findings – which mainly consisted of points of improvement.

The leader of the research program, Dr. Suresh Srivastva, encouraged Cooperrider to look beyond the points of improvement and to focus his analysis and feedback on the positive aspects of collaboration he had found within the hospital during his inquiry.

This novel approach triggered a powerful response: interest in Cooperrider's reports increased dramatically and other groups of employees agreed to participate in appreciative interviews on their work as well. They focused on questions such as: What makes you proud? What is going well and why? These sessions led to animated conversations on the hospital's future ambitions and sparked new plans and ideas for improvement. Talking about what works well and what we are proud of, apparently resulted in energy for change and renewal (Tjepkema & Verheijen, 2012).

Inspired by these results, the Cleveland Clinic was the first large organization to embark on a large-scale inquiry into those features that are life-giving to a system: positive elements that generate energy and inspire people. The term Appreciative Inquiry first appeared in a footnote in the report written by Cooperrider and Srivastva for the Board of the Cleveland Clinic. The research sequel is Cooperrider's PhD thesis, supervised by Srivastva. In his thesis, *Appreciative Inquiry: Toward a Methodology for Understanding and Enhancing Organizational Innovation* (1986), Cooperrider articulated the foundations and rationale of AI. A year later, the two published an article titled "Appreciative Inquiry in Organizational Life" (Cooperrider and Srivastva, 1987). Many consider this to be the "Big Bang" of Appreciative Inquiry as a change philosophy (Magruder, Watkins & Mohr, 2001).

DEVELOPMENT AND DIVERSITY

Since its beginning, AI has been welcomed in many places as an additional perspective on learning and change. The number of publications on the subject has increased significantly over the past years and includes both case studies and methodologies by practitioners as well as scientific studies.

Even though the change philosophy emerged in the context of organizational development, there are countless examples of the application of AI as a framework for personal, team and organizational development. Books such as *Appreciative Coaching* (Orem et al., 2007) and *VuurWerkt (Fire Works – in Dutch only,* Bouwen and Meeus, 2011) translate the principles and methodology of AI to the field of personal coaching and individual career counselling. *Appreciative Team Building* (Whitney et. al., 2004) focuses specifically on team development using AI. *Appreciative Leadership* (Whitney & Trosten-Bloom, 2010) zooms in on leadership based on AI principles.

It is possible to apply AI principles in a small team on a focused question, as well as in a large organization around a strategic theme. You can address a strictly operational question with an AI approach, or a tough issue that requires years of work. There are many examples of the application of AI for the transformation of large communities and cities: ranging from the Flemish/Dutch AI learning networks, the process of drafting a new constitution in Nepal and socio-economic regional development in Brazil to the global project Business as an Agent for World Benefit – a worldwide inquiry into how companies can contribute to a better world and prosper economically at the same time…. Differences in scale and context clearly require methodological creativity and tailoring, but these examples show that many variations of the practical application of AI's underlying principles are possible.

This book focuses on questions and issues from everyday working life in organizations. No matter the scale or scope of a potential change or development effort, an appreciative, inquiring approach to the conversation at hand is the way to begin. We will frequently use examples from such everyday situations or contexts and focus on the role of the leader or manager as change agent, but we will also address some more deliberate and larger change efforts.

A NEW LOGIC FOR NEW QUESTIONS

A commonly understood law in the development of novel concepts of organizations and change is that they only become mainstream when they coincide with a need for a different approach. For example, the idea of the learning organization was identified in the nineteen seventies and researched by academics such as Chris Argyris, but only embraced on a larger scale in the early nineteen nineties. At that time, the need to speed up innovation became relevant for a much larger group of organizations. In this light, it is interesting to reflect on AI in current times. What makes AI an attractive change philosophy for organizations, their leaders, and for consultants of innovation and change in this day and age?

AND, AND, AND... INCREASING COMPLEXITY

The current world of globalization is one in which contradictions reign. On the one hand the world feels like a global village and we can be surprised by the ease with which children make contact through social media. Many children in Belgium and the Netherlands for example, speak English even before they've had any lesson in that language, because they pick it up from their favorite "You Tubers". On the other hand, we all experience that many things are difficult to comprehend. For example, it is more and more unclear where and how decisions are made about things that concern us all – and what impact developments in other parts of the world have on our work and existence. In this constantly changing world, everything seems somehow connected and yet no one thing seems to change anything. Besides globalization, there is a parallel draw towards small and local: neighborhoods that come together to arrange day care, supermarkets that start selling locally produced fruits. Both movements exist side-by-side, though they appear to be contradictory to one another.

In the management of organizations these experiences of "and ...and" also present themselves. A school leader, for example, needs to plan as effectively and efficiently as possible, in order to maximize the use of available resources, such as classroom space, finances, teachers' time... There is a clear quality and monitoring process to guide this process, based on KPIs such as ratios for student performance, diplomas and absenteeism. On the other hand, it is *just as* important that this same school leader looks out for the community spirit in the school; teacher wellbeing; for keeping up with the fast-changing ⎫ leadership job descriptions and professional skills in demand on the labor market and ⎭ what that means for the curriculum... In essence, these types of tasks appear to be quite divergent and call on quite different abilities and types of attention. At times we call the first set of tasks management and the second, leadership. Viewing the school leader's Outlook calendar demonstrates how these two types of tasks are intermingled during the working day. It is an analysis made by many organizational theorists nowadays: organizations need to be both efficient *and* flexible *and* innovative *and* perform with respect for their setting and environment... and ...and, and even more, if that's possible. We need both the KPIs and spreadsheets *and* the storytelling and real conversations on the work floor.

Mainly due to this "and, and ...and dynamic," there is an increasing acknowledgement that the old singular recipes no longer work. The dominant model of planning and control often provides more an *illusion* of functionality than actual functionality (Stacey, 2010). The familiar Plan, Do, Check, Act is more and more difficult to keep up in that order. Separating the roles of analysts, decision makers and doers is often unhelpful or even impossible, because information flows unpredictably. All in all, many managerial systems provide us with the uncomfortable feeling of never catching up with reality. Studies of the successes of large planned change projects in organizations reveal that shockingly few actually achieve the envisioned objectives (Kotter, 2007).

WHICH APPROACH WORKS?

Ever more managers experience that the trusted logic of management and change programs is not well suited to address current complex questions and/or feel ill-fitted to the way they personally *want* to work. These managers are looking for a different, more expedient way of working that leads to actual change and that allows them to engage their staff in co-writing the organizational story. Professor Jan Rotman's (2014) postulates that we are not living in an era of change, but rather in a change of era which calls for more than doing things differently within the same logic. It calls for a different way of thinking and looking at changing, managing and organizing.

In his publications on complexity theory, Ralph Stacey (Stacey, 1996) suggests that questions featuring a relatively low level of uncertainty and a high degree of likely consensus about what needs to happen, benefit from a directive approach: establishing procedures; project management; setting clear targets and well-defined performance indicators. Questions or issues that are highly unpredictable and are likely to invite large differences in opinions, require a very different approach. Making a conscious choice for which approach to follow for a specific issue is becoming increasingly important.

Academics David Snowden and Mary Boone (2007) introduced the Cynefin-model, which is helpful in this regard. Cynefin, (Welsh, pronounced ku-*nev*-in) encompasses "the whole of features in our environment and experience that influence us and in ways we will never fully understand". They conclude that it is increasingly essential that managers use the "appropriate" frame to understand problems and questions. A simple problem with clear cause and effect relations can be resolved with straight forward planning and detailed process maps. However, a complex question requires a totally different approach: searching, "accepting the not-knowing." It is essential to continuously re-examine the understanding of a question. Shifting and reframing it, so as not to simplify it. The Cynefin model presupposes the capacity to combine different ways of working in an organization. For example: applying a strict protocol for the fairly predictable budgeting process while at the same time using a round table dialogue process to investigate employee satisfaction – which is a much more multi-faceted and complex issue.

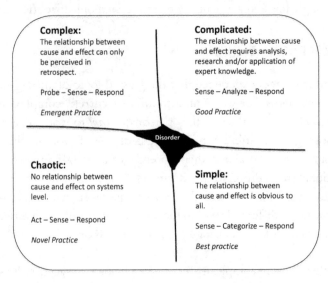

Cynefin David Snowden and Mary Boone, 2007

SWITCHING PERCEPTIONS: ORGANIZATION OR ORGANIZING?

The difference between an approach for simple issues and one for complex questions does not only concern the application of different methods. It is more a matter of changing perspectives: a different view on what an organization is and how change happens. An organization can be approached as a machine, a structure in which you designate assignments and implement any necessary changes, but it can also be understood as a group of people, working and collaborating on a specific task. Thus, an organization can be described as a web of human relationships which is shaped and reshaped on a daily basis. When we see organizations in this light, we basically regard them not as a structure, but as a process; not an organization but *an organizing*.

In the notion of an organization, change is a transition from one level of status quo to the next level. Organizational researchers Gervase Bushe and Robert Marshak (2015) call this the *diagnostic change model*. In this perspective, organizational change starts with diagnosing the bottleneck and its origins and replacing it with an alternative, more effective, approach. Repairing what is wrong. Approached from the viewpoint of an organizing, change is a process of development. In this perspective, the organization is constructed step by step, day by day. Every action, every conversation helps shape it and bring it into being. The organization is nothing more or less than the combination of all of these human (inter)actions. In this perspective, change starts by people in the organization creating a shared understanding of their current way of working and generating images of their desired future. That is why Bushe and Marshak call this a *dialogical change approach* (Bushe & Marshak, 2015). Neither of these two perspectives is truer than the other, but they do differ fundamentally. The process or development perspective (organizing) is more suited to complex and chaotic questions than the machine and management perspective (organization).

This brings us to the issue of leadership. What is the purpose of leadership in a dynamic, dialogic perspective of organizing? In this book we adopt a more relational vision of leadership than the quest for unique qualities of the leader-hero or heroine. In this perspective, leadership is about building strong relations in a group, in such a way that it moves along as an agile whole; enabling everyone, including the leader, to be at their best. This implies taking care of the conversational space, creating powerful connections, an atmosphere of trust and the development of a cooperative capacity (Fry & Barrett, 2005). In this type of leadership, it is more about a well-formulated question than about the delivery of an all-too simple answer that is not shared or understood by everyone. It is more about creating connectedness and an inquiring conversation that enables everyone to exchange future images, rather than directive, solution-driven management. And it is more about experimenting together, than about detailed marching orders. Appreciative Inquiry provides tangible inspiration for such a dynamic approach to leadership.

APPRECIATIVE INQUIRY AS A PERSPECTIVE

The theory of Appreciative Inquiry is based on a seemingly straightforward assumption: if you want something to change, start by changing the conversations. This premise reveals a social-constructionist perspective of organizations as processes of organizing. Human systems, such as teams and organizations, tend to develop themselves in the direction of their recurring questions, dominant narratives, topics of joint reflection. A compelling and positive first question triggers change processes when it drives joint inquiry and learning, leading people to adapt their practices and behaviors.

APPRECIATIVE, INQUIRING, PARTICIPATIVE AND GENERATIVE

An AI process is consistently focused on what people want to see more of. That is what is intended by *appreciative*. The inquiry is therefore always based on a positive theme, such as satisfied customers or flawless customer service – and never on a problem or deficit-based question such as: how do we reduce the number of customer complaints? A problem might very well be a trigger to *start* an AI process, but the diagnosis and focus is consistently on the strengths and capabilities within a system, both as a gateway to finding new ideas for development and as a catalyst for strengthening the relationships between people.

The *inquiring* nature of AI is about learning. In the sense of creating a better understanding of processes and practices by a cycle of carefully reflecting on experiences, deriving possible next steps, curiously watching how things unfold and then designing next steps again. AI processes are not highly planned, but rather more improvisational in nature; driven by wonder and curiosity.

AI is also a very *participatory* way of working. The group shapes the necessary change or innovation together, by doing. Rather than a strict hierarchical structure, it is about co-creation: a process in which it is often difficult to pinpoint where reflection ends and action starts, as both strongly feed into each other. By exploring the central question, generative energy and ideas come up and seamlessly transition into collaborative action. In a very organic way, people take it upon themselves to take initiative for new experiments.

That is an important feature of AI: it is a *generative* way of working. Meaning that it leads to positive energy and increased self-confidence that enables decision-making and action planning. At the end of a well-executed multi-stakeholder Appreciative Inquiry, people have new ideas and are also highly motivated to bring those ideas into being. Typically, group relations are also strengthened during the dialogue process, which in itself contributes to swift action. Mutual trust and group efficacy increase when people have joint positive images, shared experiences and ambitions.

PAST, FUTURE, TRANSITION

When speaking of change, our conversations usually gravitate towards what has to be new, different or improved in the future. In that light AI is different, because here, we first turn to the *past* to connect with strengths, best practices and success factors – things that won't change but that can be leveraged to foster any desired change. Then, images of the best possible *future* are explored, after which the attention is shifted to what is needed to *move* in the direction of that desired future.

The idea behind AI as a change philosophy is that an organization is basically a system that is continuously moving and developing. Every change is thus no more and no less than a new episode that builds on and flows from earlier developments and previous conversations. All organizations have something valuable – things that are life-giving – in their past. When these features are placed in the core of the change process, as a base to build on and work from, change becomes a positive experience without unnecessary resistance and with fewer feelings of disruption. In an AI approach the past is honored and the new is approached as something to look forward to, making it more natural to embrace any steps that are necessary to move in that direction (Cooperrider et al, 2003, AI Handbook). To sum it up: within AI we work with three elements that are equally important to ensure a successful change effort: the sustainable, the new and the transition.

The Sustainable: What Do We Want to Keep?

The opening question used in AI is generally not about what the new should be; rather it is about where we stand now and what has brought us to where we are today. In other words: what are the strengths we want to maintain, as we are about to embark on a change journey? What has already helped us to be at our best? What are we building on? This is the point of departure.

This way of thinking is both reassuring and energizing. The mere idea that there are elements worth keeping and maintaining in times of change has a positive, reassuring influence. Also, the underlying premise that change is not (only) sought after because things are wrong – but because it is necessary or desired to work towards a better future, sets a positive tone. Generally, it is reassuring to be able to build on what is known and has been achieved in the past. Therefore, by explicitly addressing the strengths and power already present, it is easier to generate challenging images for the future. This first phase is all about looking back in order to make steps forward.

The New: Images of the Most Desired Future, a Beckoning Perspective

The second dimension is the innovation. The organization positions itself for new opportunities and asks the question: What are we able to do together? People create images of their most desired future. They express and exchange wishes and ideals and combine individual ambitions into collective dreams.

The Transition: Creating a Route to the Future

The third element of the change process is shaping the envisioned future: undertaking new initiatives, using the strengths already present and building on effective experiences. It is about intentionally moving towards the new situation, step by step; by embarking on first experiments, by adopting an iterative design approach, or in more free-flowing improvisation.

Thus, the inquiry in AI does not only focus on a system's strengths and wishes for the future, but also on how to actually create this future: *What* are we going to *do together?* This is the more active, experimental phase of inquiry, while the first is more reflective and analytical.

WHAT DOES AN APPRECIATIVE INQUIRY PROCESS LOOK LIKE?

Appreciative Inquiry is not so much a technique or method for change; it is rather a processual perspective on change. Hence, no two appreciative inquiries are identical in nature. One can design a stand-alone AI type intervention, and shape one's daily management practice on these principles. The key is to apply the basic philosophy and tailor your approach or intervention to a specific context and situation (Tjepkema & Kabalt, 2012).

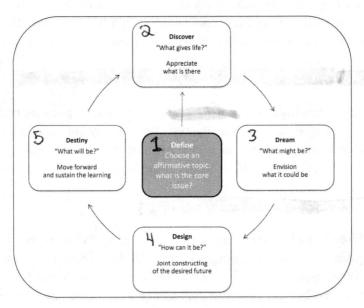

Appreciative Inquiry 5D-cycle

A common representation of an appreciative inquiry process is the 5D-cycle. It starts with identifying the *affirmative topic*: the positive theme or question that will be at the heart of the inquiry (Define). Subsequent steps include uncovering what can be learned from positive past experiences with this topic (Discovery), envisioning how things could be if the topic would be realized at its best and fullest (Dream), considering what needs to be done and identifying promising opportunities to move in the desired direction (Design), and identifying and enacting upon detailed plans for next steps (Destiny) (see i.e. Masselink et al, 2008; Masselink et al 2011; Tjepkema & Verheijen, 2009).

This model offers a general idea of the dynamics or types of conversations within an AI-process and provides a roadmap for a possible design of the process. However, it is not meant as a detailed set of steps that always need to be followed or applied – there are many AI-trajectories that just focus on one or two of the Ds.

According to Gervase Bushe (2005) the cycle combines (integrates) two types of inquiry: a reflective (Define, Discover, Dream) and an active type (Design, Destiny). The first is a more narrative and explorative inquiry with the intent to construct a *relational space*. Here encountering, grounding and deepening take center stage. The second type concerns experimental inquiry, focusing on activity and experimentation in an *action space*.

In addition, the time required for completing a full appreciative inquiry can vary. Some take place during a two or even three-day meeting in which all the Ds are subsequently addressed (an AI Summit). Others are organized as a string of meetings, spread out over time, with every meeting addressing part of the process. There are many possibilities.

Below, we will describe the different phases or steps in more detail.

DEFINE: WHAT ARE WE GOING TO INVESTIGATE?

The first step is truly essential to define the core focus of the inquiry. In AI, this is what is called the Affirmative Topic. This is the theme that takes center stage and provides direction to the inquiry. It is basically an aspiration statement as it captures where people want to go and what they want more of. Defining this focus is of the utmost importance because it centers and focusses the process.

It is called an affirmative topic or theme instead of goal, because it is often not a well-defined point or state – but rather something that still needs to be investigated and refined, not a SMART target that either can be reached or not.

It is important that the core theme has a positive focus and is not accidently a flipped problem. Many change objectives are (unconsciously) negatively framed, such as: a 10% reduction in complaints about the visitor reception. Such a statement *sounds* like a goal, but in reality, it is nothing more than a reversal of a current problem (visitors are complaining). An affirmative topic could be, for example, a positive welcoming experience for all visitors. It expresses what you *want* in a way that you can almost (but not quite yet) envision it.

An appreciative inquiry focuses on what is essential to the people in a system, on what they want more of. Sometimes, the first step is that participants or stakeholders need to reframe a problem in such a way that possibilities become visible. For instance, by investigating the hidden desire behind it: You want the number of complaints to diminish… Tell me, if the complaints would disappear, what would it look like? How would people behave differently? What would they do? What would they say? And what would be the effect? What would make that important or valuable to you?

In this first process of defining the topic, many things happen immediately, because people engage in joint discussion of what they really want to happen. They explore and exchange what is behind current problems in terms of ambitions, drive and vision. As a consequence, discussions about the causes of the problem between different groups in the organization (the mechanics have a different perception from that of their team leader, location X thinks like this, location Y sees it like that…) tend to disappear into the background. Debate makes way for dialogue, as people leave their entrenched positions and defensive reactions behind and enter into a genuine exchange about possibilities.

This positive framing establishes a foundation for discovering new perspectives. In one instance, a school battling increasing drop-out rates, chose to investigate why dissatisfied and vulnerable students who were about to leave or drop-out, actually remained *on board*. This led to really different insights than previous projects that had focused on students who left and their reasons for dropping out. Understanding what made vulnerable students stay, enabled the development of effective approaches to help more of them finish school.

The following criteria are useful to check your affirmative topic:

- Is the subject stated affirmatively?
- Does it express a desire?

- Does it have a relational dynamic; is it a beckoning perspective for the different parties concerned?

- Does it evoke genuine curiosity and enthusiasm?

- Does it answer to the question: Where will we stand after we have completed the journey?

Another important consideration in the Define phase is who else to involve in the subsequent steps of the AI cycle. Possible helpful questions in this regard are: Who can help us learn more about this topic? Who do we need to truly innovate on this subject or theme? Who is most likely to be impacted by changes that will happen when we start exploring this topic?

DISCOVER: GLIMPSES AND SEEDLINGS

The Discover phase is all about exploring the positive core and identifying what gives life: What are our best experiences around this theme/topic to date? Participants enter into conversations with their own anecdotes, share examples and success stories, and thus they uncover their shared success DNA. The essence here is to engage in joint strength finding, so that those concerned can apply these strengths in the future and further expand them. Conversations that are focused on what is going well, contribute to a shared understanding and positive feeling about what the organization (or team) is capable of. This builds collective confidence: Yes, we can do this!

For instance, a team that wants to improve its teamwork might share and explore past moments during which their collaboration was optimal, or an organization that wants to work on improving client experience might seek to identify and understand prior situations in which clients were most satisfied. It is not necessarily about experiences that were objectively measured as a success or could be officially labelled as best practices. Rather, it is important that the people participating in the inquiry identify their *own* stories of collaboration and client satisfaction that energized *them*, made them proud, left them with a sense of fulfilment or in other ways, make them want more of this.

In this context, a powerful concept is the *positive exception*. In the case of AI in a situation characterized by problems (i.e. low client satisfaction or poor collaboration) there are bound to be many negative examples. With an appreciative interview in the Discovery phase, people are explicitly invited not to look at the nine failed attempts, but at that one occasion in which all the pieces came together. That one story of which they say: I wish it could always be like that. In this way the spotlight is put on those experiences that would otherwise be by-passed or taken for granted. These experiences, though scarce, hold valuable information.

DREAM: WHAT FUTURE DO WE WANT?

Pausing to recall successes, identifying moments that worked and understanding more deeply how this was achieved, almost always leads to thinking about the future: How could we do more of this? What innovation is possible? How would we truly want ... to be?

During the Dream-phase people share these images and visions of the future. They act them out in such a way that the dreams really come to life. By using collages, film or video clips or little skits they create new stories and present them to each other. In this phase, it is not about identifying the single or best dream that everybody can fully endorse. Rather, the aim is to fill the space with images and ideas of what might be. Inevitably this implies that there will be multiple images or narratives. It is not about creating one collective dream, but about creating attractive futures that have the inspirational power to pull us forward.

DESIGN: DETERMINING THE WAY FORWARD

To create a focus for action, the next step is choosing opportunity areas and formulating an ambition for each of them. Opportunity areas are domains people want to work on in order to move toward the most attractive future images they have developed in the Dream phase. These are new topics and steps that will move the system forward. In recent years it has become common to apply *design-thinking* methods in this process. Brainstorming or ideation followed by co-creating and building prototypes is a very powerful manner of bridging the present with the future. Along with designing ways to pursue opportunity areas, participants may also be invited to formulate a provocative proposition for their selected area. Such a proposition is a concise and appealing image of the future for a given period, based on the dream. If your dream is ...., where will you be in x months? What will be true and expresses your deepest hopes and ambitions concerning this design topic?

Formulating the provocative proposition – or possibility statement – in the present tense (it is now January and we are …) creates the strongest appeal and combines excitement with a sense of achievement.

DESTINY: GETTING TO WORK

The last step is the enacting of plans and designs that will realize the formulated ambition (proposition statements). What are we to do (now)? Who do we need to engage with next? People formulate concrete activities and experiments, and they get to work. It is important that in this last phase, the participatory, co-creative nature of the process is kept up. There is a danger here that project management practices take process ownership away from participants. Managers often view this phase as the most challenging. It is out of the comfort zone of traditional command and control leadership, so anxiety may emerge from a lack of control over the final outcome. However, it is not about letting go, rather it is about *going with*, and leadership is very much needed. It just looks different.

The key question is: How can we create space for unusual actions that move us in the direction of the co-created future images related to the core theme? How can we, in practical terms, shape and act on our initial ideas for the future? Leadership is then about the establishment of conditions for rapid positive change. Bushe and Fry speak of track and fan in this respect. To them, leadership in this phase is about attentively monitoring what happens and which initiatives emerge and carefully considering which little fires need to be fanned to give them more oxygen to grow.

The worst thing that can happen in this phase is that a manager or organization treats the ideas or prototypes as nothing more than a set of recommendations. This is a short cut to a standstill. For leaders embracing the AI process, it is essential to foster dreams, encourage ideas, and work along with staff in realizing action plans. Only then does it become possible to look back to determine: What works? What should we pursue? How do we proceed?

COMING FULL CIRCLE

The AI cycle can then begin anew. AI has an improvisational character. Every action elicits further reflection, during which you discover new strengths (discovery) leading to new images of what is possible (dream) and these lead to renewed experimentation (design and destiny).

BASIC PRINCIPLES OF APPRECIATIVE INQUIRY

As we have stated previously, Appreciative Inquiry is used in very different settings, and there are many ways of working with it. This may range from large scale work conferences or AI summits with citizens, board members, employees and managers who jointly work on a question or issue, to short and to-the point meetings on the work floor where operators are concerned with a quality issue. In all its diversity AI is characterized by six fundamental principles that underscore all interventions and explain their effectiveness. They are often considered to be the heart of AI. We will briefly discuss them and subsequently, we endeavor to explain the active components of each of these principles.

CONSTRUCTIONIST PRINCIPLE

AI is rooted in social-constructionist theory, in which the basic principle is that we create our reality with our language. *Words create worlds.* There is not one determined or given universal reality outside of ourselves, in which we live. Rather, we construct it, jointly, through our human interaction and the manner in which we think and speak about it. By changing our manner of conversing, our perception changes and consequently, our reality changes too. Similarly, the questions we pose determine what we see and what we articulate together, and therefore influence what we are able to create.

A team of teachers did not agree with the changes that had been implemented at the school during the past years. They missed their old familiar ways of working and found the new Board and its approach to be too business-like and impersonal. They did not believe in the new educational direction and felt left out from the entire process. They frequently discussed this amongst each other in such a way that they continuously confirmed each other's grudges and reinforced each other's stories with similar anecdotes. Over time, the team became entangled in a negative conversation and a depreciative imagery of its management. This had far reaching implications. Newly joined junior staff quickly became disenchanted with the negative atmosphere in the team, people lost hope and energy, and faith in the leadership reached an all-time low.

After several fruitless attempts to turn the process around (but the new manage-ment is surely not all bad?), a new team leader decided to radically change the conversation. She agreed with the team that – as an experiment – the team meetings would no longer delve into negative stories on management or the change process. Rather, she chose to keep these meeting points short and to focus only on those issues that were clearly within the circle of influence of the team. In this way a significant part of the meetings was devoted to topics such as a joint approach to the use of mobile phones in class or providing support to a specific vulnerable student. In addition, she introduced a series of conversations about strengths: What is your strength as a teacher? How do you manage to show that talent successfully? and so on.

Slowly but surely, the mood lifted. In actual practice not much had changed – the Board and the change process were still there – but because team members could see the school, their work, and each other in a new light, there was a surge in creativity and motivation. Teachers had the feeling that the team had changed because the conversations had altered. And a more generative space emerged in which they could finally discuss the educational change process with each other in a productive way.

POETIC PRINCIPLE

Organizations are human creations. We co-create them, and they are never finished. Organizations are an ongoing story, so the question becomes: What new chapter are we going to write with each other?

A team that was frozen in their inability to collaborate, due to endless clashes and conflicts, found a new space to co-operate by making a history timeline together; a factual reconstruction of their past history as a team (high and low points) and how this was experienced by those involved. At the end, when the question about what next step they wanted to make together was raised, a surprising answer emerged: We need to get to know each other better, on a more personal level. Everyone agreed to this and plans for a small party and a team outing were made. If either of these initiatives had been a suggestion or directive by the team leader, it would never have been embraced by the whole team. But because the team came up with it together, as a logical next chapter in their story, they were all up for it.

PRINCIPLE OF SIMULTANEITY

Change starts at the very moment we ask a question. Long before we have the answers or start implementing new ideas. The inquiry sets the change in motion, and as such, is a very powerful intervention.

The management team of a financial institution wanted to improve their collaboration by adopting faster decision-making processes, shorter and more efficient meetings, and increasing their mutual support. The idea was to start with small experiments. The simple design question: "What new behavior would we like to see and what experiments do we set up to achieve this?" led to interesting conversations and a discovery process that lasted for three months. What new behavior do we really expect? What focus do we need? And what type of structure do we need to enable the desired behavior? Following this explorative phase, the organization was prepared for the first experiments in practice. However, during the initial lead up, many events or changes had already occurred, some of which surpassed initial expectations. By avoiding the vocabulary of should we change or not and using questions geared towards how do we collaborate together, energy for renewal emerged and people began to approach work, and each other, differently.

ANTICIPATORY PRINCIPLE

Positive images of a possible future are very powerful. Their appeal to people can compel them to start moving in the direction of that image or envisioned future. The beckoning horizon of the image is a catalyst for change.

Coaches sometimes pose the miracle question to their clients: Imagine that, this weekend, a miracle will happen at work, turning everything into how you would like it to be. What would that look like if you show up for work on Monday morning? Describe the picture to me. What do you see in front of you? What is happening? What has come to an end, to closure? What do you do? What are others doing? What are they saying? They help their clients paint an exact and vivid picture. Envisioning that image of a possible reality on a very concrete level literally provides direction and motivates people to start realizing this ideal future.

POSITIVITY PRINCIPLE

Positive and hopeful emotions, such as self-confidence and optimism, create energy and mobilize for action. Research of positive emotions shows how invigorating these are in increasing personal capacities, establishing relations with others, and moving into collaborative action.

> *The staff of the Communication department of a Dutch government institution had already been in a change process for two years. The intention was that they would develop from content expert to a partner role. This gave many of them the feeling that their past performance had not been good enough. During a departmental off-site meeting, the members were invited to analyze their strengths and discuss the occasions during which they were able to – in their own way – fulfil their new role successfully. Identifying strengths and fruitful examples of enacting the preferred future generated so much energy and positive emotion that in the following months they made significant progress in developing a new way of working.*

NARRATIVE PRINCIPLE

There is something magical in the sharing of stories. Stories give color and depth, they provide recognition and a sense of connectedness, and they provide meaning and give perspective. A story conveys insights and understanding that dates, facts and data cannot. Above all, stories connect people by giving them the feeling that they are part of a larger whole. Sharing personal narratives relates general knowledge through personal experiences, and this invites even more storytelling from others. Where debate or statements activate the brain to look for a counter argument or stance, a story sets the brain on a path of looking for similar experiences. Just think, if someone tells you that they have been on holiday to France, what is the first image that emerges in your mind? Or take a party conversation, during which you speak of your hernia, what reactions – besides compassion – do you get from others? Chances are that they share stories of medical problems as well.

> *Six months ago, the entire management of a bank had entered a culture change trajectory. They developed a considerable vocabulary on the desired behavior: letting go, activating staff, encouraging individual responsibility. The management team had a clear presentation about the future that was summa-*

rized powerfully and concisely in a set of core values for the envisaged culture. Nobody was against this direction and plan. However, it was obvious that there was a lack of energy in the entire process. A meeting during which they shared personal experiences on what each of them was seeking to let go of, however small was a breakthrough occasion. What did you do? What was the impact? What made it difficult? Stories started flowing, one tale triggered the next. All of a sudden everyone realized the impact they collectively had in the bank, by how they approached colleagues differently and all in their own unique way. They decided, there and then, to set up a peer-to-peer platform where they could share these experiences, serving as a driver of the culture change.

REFLECTIVE QUESTIONS FROM THE PRINCIPLES

- Reflect on an example (from your own or somebody else's experience) that illustrates how something grows, expands or improves if you give it attention.

- Think back to a time when you were an integral part of a radical shift or turn of direction, in a group, team or organization – as if you wrote a next chapter together. What happened?

- Reflect on an example in which you actively embraced a new question or a shift of the question and in hindsight this appeared to be the most important intervention.

- Describe a time when you were inspired by someone's images of a desired future or by co-creating images with others (in the literal sense or in the form of metaphors).

- Recall one of your best days at work – you (and perhaps others) were filled with positive emotions. Describe what happened and how the positive emotions influenced your behaviors.

- Think of a time when you truly felt part of a larger whole or body. How did that come about? What impact did it have on you?

APPRECIATIVE INQUIRY AND ORGANIZATIONAL CHANGE: BASIC COMPONENTS

Together, the core principles discussed above contain the four essential components that capture the essence of the AI perspective on change:

- a focus on generativity
- inquiry as the sustainable element
- building relational practices
- appreciating what is there

A FOCUS ON GENERATIVITY (AND THE ROLE OF POSITIVITY)

A dominant critique of AI in recent years concerns a presumed exclusive focus on the positive. According to a number of authors (i.e. Bushe, 2007) it was unclear how important positivity was for the success of AI. Others suggested that AI ignores a large share of organizational reality, as it merely focuses on positive stories. It is our belief that this is more due to the focus of certain applications of AI than to the theory itself. Nevertheless, this discussion yielded an important insight: the need to emphasize the importance of *generativity* in AI processes.

The intention of an AI perspective on change is that the change process generates new ideas *and* motivation amongst those concerned (the different stakeholders) to extend their collaboration so that those ideas can be put into practice. In other words, people develop new approaches together and the process of developing those plans energizes and motivates them to realize these initiatives collaboratively. The essence of AI is encouraging generative connections between people that lead to new possibilities and shared enthusiasm to turn those images into action. This energy is not only present in the ideas but is also contained and sustained in the relationships. The AI process strengthens the connections between those involved, which in itself, motivates them to continue working together. The connection thus becomes generative. Whenever we ask people what their feelings are after a one-on-one interview using an AI interview guide, they respond in terms of being or feeling connected, happy, energized, or hopeful. Such positive emotions are a pre-condition for generative connections.

This phenomenon is easily experienced during an AI Summit, a two or three-day meeting of a diverse group of stakeholders who work together on a question that they want to take forward. Very seldom do participants join or attend these sessions to get more work assigned to them. But it is our experience that many leave the summit with new action roles and assignments that they chose themselves. AI in its magical best creates generative conversations, so people voluntarily step up and take ownership (Fry & Barrett, 2005).

Thus, the focus on the positive in AI is not about the denial of negative elements or experiences; rather, it has to do with the question of how to arrange conversations in such a way that they increase the possibility that people conclude that conversation with a positive and connected feeling that compels further action together. It is very difficult to truly establish a generative connection based upon conversations that trigger negative emotions.

In their article that first framed AI, David Cooperrider and Suresh Srivastva suggested that Appreciative Inquiry is generative (Zandee, 2013); it creates more hope and confidence in the human capacity to jointly create something wonderful and because of that, it inspires us to act upon it. Generative connections are both input for, and the result of, the manner in which we converse with each other within AI.

INQUIRY AS THE SUSTAINABLE ELEMENT

Organizational life is brimming with questions: Why is our staff turnover so high? How should we adapt to the changing market? How can we increase client satisfaction? Why is the second production line less efficient? Can we collaborate more effectively across our locations?

These questions are, in part, expressions of a drive or at least an urgency to be more efficient, to grow, to be good or become even better. As such, they form the root of all learning, and therefore are essential for the development of every team and every organization.

But in order to support this drive, it is important to move beyond the measurable or quantitative questions such as: What is the average employee satisfaction rate? Those questions have a very different impact from questions like: When are our employees most satisfied with their job? Or, to phrase it differently: How can we turn this organization into a place where everybody comes to work with a smile? The first question is less enticing than the other two. Questions focus and attract our attention and shape the direction of the exchange.

Posing powerful *affirmative* questions that generate energy and provoke positive change is at the core of AI as a perspective on change. Collective inquiry around such questions drives change and transformation. Therefore, AI calls for a consistent mode of curiosity to question what drives and energizes us or others to pursue what we truly desire to create.

> *We felt the power of affirmative questions very strongly in a learning program with a group of managers. The program was designed to answer learning questions of participants, who were all first-time managers. Basically, all their questions boiled down to their performance in their new role: How can I perform well as a manager? How do I meet the standards? Approaches were unique. Some wanted to learn how to discover and use their employee's strengths. Others were concerned with encouraging strong and effective team collaboration or with deploying plans more systematically. But the underlying quest was very similar.*

> *Near the end of the trajectory, this started to shift. We shared our observation with the group by pointing out that we sensed a different, underlying question leading their conversations. The dominant question we could hear in between the lines was no longer: "How can I perform well?" but had become: "How can I do good as a manager?" Basically, participants' attention had shifted from an effectiveness issue to a purposing question. Realizing that this was indeed the case, had a profound effect on these managers. It gave more depth to their individual learning processes, deepened the dialogue and personal conversations and strengthened their mutual relations. The entire process received a boost when it turned into a more intentional search focused on doing "good", in order to then perform well.*

Finally, the inquiring and dialogic nature of AI also suggests that nobody can monopolize the truth. Several story lines can exist side-by-side and no single expert can possibly know *the* truth. In short, it's not about who holds the truth or who is right, but it concerns the question: In what reality do *we* want to live or work? What shared image do *we* aspire to? How do *we* perceive what is most important to us? Appreciating and activating this intention to continue inquiring is of importance to establish and maintain generative connections.

RELATIONAL PRACTICES

The starting point for AI is that organizations are networks of relationships that have infinite possibilities. At times, during workshops or learning sessions on AI, we use a movie clip from the documentary Landfill Harmonic. It is the story of a community in Latin America who live and work on and around a garbage dumpsite and who make their living by separating and selling garbage. At one point in time, one of the men found a violin case and this inspired him to make musical instruments. Others joined his plan, and using basic materials such as oil drums, forks, metal strings, tin cans, cases, bolts, pieces of wood they constructed violins, drums, even a cello and trumpets. This then attracted people with musical talents, who managed to produce beautiful, magical music with these instruments. Eventually, this led to the establishment of a music school and an orchestra that, following the release of the documentary, now plays concerts all over the world. The community spirit, resourcefulness and musicality of all this is startling, humbling and inspiring: an emergent symphony of strengths, borne from curiosity and creativity, within one-on-one relationships. A beautiful illustration of what groups of people are capable of.

In Appreciative Inquiry the primary focus of the leader is not to come up with substantive solutions – since these emerge from the group. The leader's role is to model and help develop strong relational practices: fostering connections and conversations between people that are so useful that they want to take them further, investing in them, so that new things are easily created together. In other words, the leader's job is to foster relational spaces in which people bring out the best in each other and take on responsibility.

There are many different ways in which you can support and provoke this. Such as:

- asking an inquiry question that stimulates curiosity amongst many
- encouraging the sharing of past, best case stories
- inviting people to collaborate in developing an ideal image of the future

- setting the task of co-designing a prototype

- influencing the quality and nature of the conversations

- celebrating progress after the team has made a small step in the direction of what is most important for them

THE POWER OF APPRECIATION

The focus of AI is on what gives life to a system, as Cooperrider (2003) so eloquently puts it. What gets people going? What drives them? What are their strengths? It is a natural human tendency, and indeed a practice that is built in many organizational processes, to pay attention to what goes wrong or otherwise demands corrective energy. In AI, it is not at all necessary to ignore or avoid that. Indeed, frustration and dissatisfaction with a yet-to-be-realized wish or dream is often a trigger that sets the ball rolling and lead to ground-breaking innovations. However, an appreciative inquiry steers away from a problem analysis: What is wrong? What causes the failure? It navigates the thinking and subsequent dialogue in a different direction; that of the positive core which is present in every person and human system. This core is that which gives life and forward momentum to effort(s). In the Landfill Harmonic documentary, the initiators and members of the orchestra explain how great their love of music is and how this makes their lives meaningful. With AI, we try to create movement by explicitly focusing on the positive core, even when it is disguised behind frustration, resistance or a problem situation.

To appreciate literally means seeing and working with those things present that you value or deem worthwhile. For instance:

- the different strengths and qualities in a group

- the grit and perseverance people have to endure or overcome a difficult situation

- the creative ability to think of possibilities and look for opportunities

- energizing moments in interactions

- positive experiences from the past

- an ambition or desire for a better future

Appreciative practices, such as: thinking in possibilities, outlining a desired future and sharing successes, energizes and motivates people towards action. In addition, these practices evoke positive emotions such as: joy, pride, confidence and optimism. The shared experience of these emotions is infectious. It rapidly strengthens mutual connections, propels people toward collaboration, and enables the process of finding a shared vision or purpose.

IMPLICATIONS FOR LEADERSHIP

What do these perspectives on organizing and changing mean for leadership? What is the kind of leadership that is needed to guide these processes and replace the increasingly limited, more classical archetypical image of the leader-hero? The answer can't be captured in one sentence or image, but several building blocks of a new leadership profile come to the fore.

NOT-KNOWING AS A STRENGTH

In his book *De kunst van leiderschap (2011) (The Art of Leadership – in Dutch only)* organizational expert Eric Koenen uses the image of the fallen angel. It is a painting of two servants carrying away an angel who has just fallen from heaven. For Koenen, this symbolizes the emerging change in how we view leadership. When the role of management was initially articulated by Frederick Taylor, it was literally a decision-making role. Managers were most knowledgeable on the work process, had overview and lots of experience, and were content experts. It was inconceivable for them to not know things. Those days have since passed. We no longer expect a manager or leader to know everything (though some still expect that of themselves...) (see Kessels, 2012). The increasing speed at which change occurs, the growing complexity of the world we operate in, the way in which information flows – it all makes it impossible for one person to know everything. There is not one single correct mode of operation. And unknowing or not-knowing becomes a potential strength. Because curiosity translates into asking questions and inquiring and leading people to find novel answers together. Doing that well – inquiring with a sense of wonder and amazement– and using that to guide organizational processes effectively is becoming a vital new art of leadership.

ORGANIZING REQUIRES MULTIPLE VOICES

Since complex questions cannot be answered by one single person, it is necessary to involve others. Generating creativity and rich ideas calls for inviting new viewpoints and many perspectives. Starting a multi-stakeholder conversation by engaging colleagues from other sections, clients, citizens, and external stakeholders requires managers to cross the borders of their own department. When drawing in more voices and ideas, at first, things will become more complex instead of simpler. That richness is needed to arrive at new shared goals and viable solutions and is something leaders can and should organize. It is important for them to be able to handle that complexity and confusion and turn it into a productive exchange.

This approach toward engaging with more of the whole of a human system implies a shift in leadership focus. It is a shift from content or expert-driven leadership to leading via multi-stakeholder relations; from *leading for* to *leading with*. This may challenge one's faith in others and their capacities. It poses leaders with a personal and profound question: Do I trust and have confidence in others such that we can realize beautiful things together? This requires leaders to have a keen eye for people's talents and strengths so that they understand what each and every one has to offer. Such a focus feeds confidence and ensures that leaders are able to select the people to join and contribute appropriately and effectively.

CONVERSATION AS THE CORE PROCESS OF ORGANIZING

The notion that an organization does not exist outside of its members, but rather consists of an intricate network of relationships between people who together create the organization on a day-to-day basis – or in other words, the lens of organizing instead of organization – implies that conversation is the core process of organizing. The role of leadership is then to influence the quality of relationships and conversations. For instance: by taking care that people understand each other, that discussions evolve into dialogues where people learn from each other, that people correctly assess developments in the outside world and jointly come up with new ideas to face these challenges and to realize joint ambitions…. Leadership is about creating strong relations and meaning-making conversations.

IN CHARGE, NOT IN CONTROL

In *The paradox of control in organizations*, Philip Streatfield (2001), points to the difference between being in charge and being in control. As manager or leader, no matter how keenly you might want to be in control, you rarely are! If organizing is the consequence of conversation, we need to realize that we only control our initial gesture (comment, directive, question, etc.). Once the other person responds, we are now in a joint act of creativity, or dance, or debate, or whatever metaphor comes to mind. Neither party is in control of the outcome of the conversation; it is now, by definition, a co-construction. So, in this sense, no single person controls the entire process of organizing and changing. In your formal role, you may be in charge of connecting people, adding themes to meetings or the agenda, determining from which question you will enter the conversation, and inviting people to express their deepest wish for the future of the organization.

INTERVIEW: WIEKE LEONHARD – CITY OF AMSTERDAM

"AN ORGANIZATION THAT IS LED BY PEOPLE WHO THINK IN TERMS OF POSSIBILITIES, WILL ACHIEVE MORE."

As senior consultant, Corporate Learning, Wieke Leonhard is concerned with Learning & Development within the municipality of Amsterdam. Prior to that, she was a project leader for the Learning Organization project at the Department of Work and Income. This was part of the New Way of Working Program and focused on continuous learning, improvement and innovation within the organization.

I got to know Appreciative Inquiry during a course on Corporate Learning. AI was treated as one of the modules, but I noticed that it also formed the basis of the whole program, we just *did* AI. I found that surprising and pleasant. The approach felt very personal, the focus was clearly on my development and growth, so I learned a lot. Based on that experience, I started to deepen my knowledge of AI. I took a course in it, started to apply AI in projects and now I give AI courses myself where I share my inspiration with others.

THE A OF AI: APPEALING TO THE AVAILABLE STRENGTH

When I think about the core of AI on the basis of these experiences, I always get back to the two words that make up its name: appreciation and inquiry. The first for me is about actively using the knowledge, expertise and energy available in an organization. Strength generates strength, people dare to do more, take initiative and deliver great results. Feeling that your talents are visible, in my opinion, is a basic need that employees want to have met in their work environment.

When I hear managers in our organization say: People don't take initiative here! I think: That can't be true! It has to do with how you approach people, and yes, you have to break the pattern that everything is imposed from above. You have to literally invite people to take the initiative and then give bottom-up ideas a chance. In places where this happens, I have seen people and teams change tremendously. An organization is more than a rational sum of processes, structures and FTEs, it is a group of people who want to do meaningful work, who want to contribute and who have ideas.

THE I OF AI: RESEARCH AS CONTINUOUS CURIOSITY

The second element of AI is the investigative one. In my role as Corporate Learning consultant, I believe that in the long term we will make progress if we remain inquisitive and curious. That's what continuous learning is about. Learning at work becomes a natural process when people have investigative skills and habits. It leads to more knowledge, more experiments, faster learning, more innovation and less operating from a single image.

The concept of organizational development is also changing. We think much more in terms of continuous development than in change as big leaps from one state to another. For me, research is more than just asking good questions. For example, it's also about daring to experiment; figuring out how something works by doing something new.

In the context of a local government such as ours, this becomes even more interesting when we involve partners and clients from outside. For example, a group of seventy civil servants talked to the people of Amsterdam about their wishes and ideas about an issue in a particular area of the city. They found this very exciting and a little bit scary. After all, as a researcher, you go on a journey without knowing exactly where you will end up. We have increased such experiences. For example, we have set up a course in which civil servants work on real issues in the city. We invite them to come up with innovative solutions in their approach with as many people as possible, from inside and outside the organization. I notice that these kinds of practices affect the role we play as local authorities. We are challenging the self-evident fact that we first have to think of everything ourselves as civil servants before we can go outside and inform people. As a result, far more citizens are now coming to us with great ideas. Things are really shifting.

RESULTS IN VARIOUS AREAS

When I was still a project leader in the Work and Income Department, I set up a facilitator's pool with nineteen colleagues who were all trained in Appreciative

Inquiry. They supported internal groups to achieve results in terms of better service and better internal operation. The key message was: be supportive researchers. And it worked. The results of the services at Work and Income have improved partly due to AI. Customer satisfaction and employee engagement have increased.

There were so many success stories that the number of questions and initiatives was unstoppable. So, whereas it was regarded with a bit of suspicion in the beginning, it really took off. And nowadays, these AI facilitators are part of an organization-wide pool that is active in a wide range of fields and departments. It has really spread.

DARING TO MAKE YOUR VOICE HEARD

What's apparent to me is that in many stories about AI in our organization, great things have started with one small brave decision. They may easily be overlooked, yet those tiny moments are so meaningful. For instance, I know of a director who made himself vulnerable in a management meeting by saying that he doesn't always know the answer either. Admitting this triggered a different discourse.

Recently, I was in a meeting with a lot of complaining about what was bad about our organization, and I pointed out that I actually also saw a lot of good things happening. That gave a new twist to the conversation. Afterwards, people came to tell me how refreshing they found my input. It is always very tempting to go along with a dominant discourse and it takes some courage to step up and say that you want or see something different. The strange thing is; it feels scary in the moment, but because you make it more personal, something good always happens.

CONTINUING TO LEARN ABOUT AI

We have set something in motion in our organization that we want to continue to learn about. AI is an integral part of our organizational development, but we don't call it that. If you put that label first, then you have to make a case for it. Very quickly, we start looking at people and approaches to see whether they are AI or not, and I don't think that's at all productive.

APPRECIATIVE INQUIRY AS A DAILY LEADERSHIP PRACTICE

I prefer to work on the basis of the basic principles rather than on the basis of the methodology. The challenge then lies in playing with and combining all kinds of approaches, in order to create something that fits in exactly with the question before us. I like to do that and think of new forms and variants. What I would really love is to get to a point with our organization where we are so adept at changing and developing that we never again have to start a formal re-organization. That would be a beautiful achievement. Then, we would be a true learning organization.

A DEEPER UNDERSTANDING: APPRECIATIVE INQUIRY WORKING PRINCIPLES

FROM A GIVEN PROBLEM TO A CHOSEN TOPIC

Whenever you want change, the reason why is the first aspect that requires attention. You might have a nagging feeling and perceive a strong need for change and you might even ask yourself: How do I convince others of this? How do I create a willingness to change in my organization? Most management literature would suggest that a sense of urgency is needed in the form of a so-called *burning platform*. In terms of Kurt Lewin's change theory (Lewin, 1951) the first phase of change is *unfreezing*: making sure that people feel the need to step into action because they perceive the current situation as unsafe or threatening. In later theories and models of change as well, for instance John Kotter's theory (Kotter, 1996) the first step is always defined as creating a sense of urgency through pointing out what is going (or about to go) wrong. In these models, a thorough analysis of the problem, its root causes and its expected negative repercussions is an important strategy to convince everybody of the fact that change is needed.

How does this work with Appreciative Inquiry? Do people want to move into action when they explore what is going well? Doesn't focusing on existing strengths and successes lead to an embrace of the status quo? How can this inquiry be done in such a way that it leads to urgency in terms of energy to get going? The way in which the *affirmative topic* is formulated is essential here. Before we explore how, let us first reflect on the unexpected side effects of working with a burning platform as a catalyst for change.

CREATING URGENCY THROUGH PROBLEM AWARENESS

This traditional approach of creating urgency through an emphasis on problem awareness contributes to a number of unwanted side effects:

- Focusing on the sources of current problems does not create new images of possibilities for the future. A possible effect of this could be that the system remains stuck in the awareness that something is not going well but lacks the understanding of what can be done differently. People may get to understand what they don't want anymore and what to avoid, but that is really not the same as knowing what you're after, or what you desire.

- With this type of problem analysis, the ownership is often not where you would like it to be; namely with the people concerned. For conducting objective analyses, an (internal or external) expert often conducts the diagnosis and develops the dominant change narrative. People might be convinced, but that is something different than feeling a true sense of ownership. You might only become aware of this later in the process, when the need for action replaces the need for thinking, or when need for compliance is replaced by the need for initiative.

- Identification and analysis of the problem often (implicitly) leads to the question of who is to blame. Whose mistake or error created this unwanted situation? At other times, fear or doubt emerges. Can we still turn the tide? Such questions have, even if they are tacit, a negative effect on existing relations and on the spirit of openness required to come up with new solutions together.

A more fundamental question concerns the premise on which the burning platform idea is based. Putting the problem in the spotlight doesn't necessarily create the impetus and energy to deal with it adequately. We experienced this first-hand in a chemical company where we assisted with a project evaluation.

On the factory grounds there were two technical production units and a large project team had recently thoroughly modernized one of these installations. The moment had come to tackle the second one. The project manager thought it was valuable to learn from the initial project, before embarking on the second one. During the first meeting all team members were invited to explore what had gone well during the first project. Things that were experienced as successful would become building blocks for the new project. In a second round, the members of the project team would be asked to brainstorm on which dimensions they could do better or what could be done differently.

One group of participants thought the question of collecting success stories was completely irrelevant. During the modernization process of the first installation several things had gone wrong, so they said that in order to avoid a repetition of mistakes, they thought it was essential to analyze these mistakes. The other groups embraced the notion of an inquiry into successful stories. Within half an hour, the difference in atmosphere and energy between the groups was remarkable. Those who were engaged with the collection and inquiry of the successes were focused. They were laughing and already had ideas for the next project phase. The group that opted to explore mistakes, showed a very different picture. Their mood had changed dramatically. The initial determination had disappeared and was replaced by a sense of resignation. Their speech volume had dropped. At a certain moment someone remarked to his colleagues: When you look at all these problems, you almost would start to question yourself. Why stay here? Why even bother? Starting with the problems of the initial project, their conversation had drifted into a feeling that the entire organization was problematic. This is an expression of the words create worlds phenomenon. By discussing a problem in a group, no matter how good and truthful the analysis is, you run the risk of stifling energy and creative spirit. Sometimes a sense of discouragement develops, when people start feel overwhelmed by the problem.

AN ALTERNATIVE MEANING: URGENCY AS A CALLING

With AI, a sense of urgency comes from a calling to pursue, not from a threat or danger to avoid. On the one hand it leans on the belief that something is so valuable that people want to sustain and build on that power as a team or as an organization. And on the other hand, it builds on a positive future image that is so powerful and attractive that people become curious and want to know more about it. The urgency becomes a calling, a theme that is formulated in such a way that you *want to be* involved and make it happen.

Of course the motive to change or renew something can be grounded in critique, a problem, danger or some other situation that is perceived as undesirable. The thought that enables us to embrace this motive is: every critique or complaint can also be viewed as an expression of an unfulfilled wish. In other words, hidden behind the feeling or expression of discontent, there lies a longing for a more desirable future. There is something at stake that people value. The art of taking an appreciative eye in such a situation is to look for that longing or desire and to twist or flip the problem in such a way that the possibilities and wishes become visible again. Just like a coin has two sides, the desired future is the reverse side of the dreaded past or present.

IDENTIFYING THE AFFIRMATIVE TOPIC

Creative and aspirational reframing is an important step in Appreciative Inquiry. With the Define phase you embark on a joint search for the affirmative topic or the desired change destination. Sometimes, it can take weeks involving many conversations with stakeholders before you can conclude together that: yes, this is the exact phrasing of what we want. At other times it goes much more quickly.

One thing is a given: you will be unable to get there by simply reversing the problem. A reversed or flipped problem is something different than an affirmative topic. A college that faced an alarming and increasing number of students who failed to graduate, initially identified 0% drop-outs as their target. That aim did not provide sufficient direction – everybody appeared to understand it differently, and many teachers could not see what it meant and felt that it was unrealistic. Above all, the goal mostly expressed a desire to solve the existing problem but did not give a real sense of what would be different in the school. Rephrasing the topic through questions as: "What do you truly want for your students?" and "What would it mean or look like if all students stay until they have graduated?" led to a more meaningful and attractive affirmative topic which was eventually articulated as: a promising study career for all.

The problem of the rising drop-out rates had been reframed. People started to think and speak about: How can we keep students that are drifting or potentially exiting, on board? How can we help them to realize a promising study career? What would that look like for them? What do we do and what do they do? This not only increased enthusiasm for the project – as everyone became curious – it also led to fresh insights. For example, people discovered that in most cases personal attention from an individual teacher made the difference for a student to remain at the college. And in other cases, students were helped to transfer to a different field of study, instead of merely dropping out.

In another setting, the initial problem of employability of older staff members became: job satisfaction for everyone. In yet another, the problem of long, indecisive meetings became: prompt decision making processes. A paralyzed workers' council opted for: a workers' council that gives people a voice and bridges the gap with management. All of these themes emerged through asking questions such as: You currently have a problem which is not what you want, can you tell me, what *do* you want? What does it look like when that problem is not there, when are you at your best? What would you want to have more of? What are your images of a desired future, to augment the stories you have about the disliked past?

Criteria for the formulation of a powerful affirmative topic or focus for an appreciative inquiry are:

- Every participant you want to invite understands the relevance and the importance of the topic

- It makes people curious and wanting to know more about it

- It works as a guiding North Star, there is excitement about the direction it suggests

- It resonates with the organization and is linked with its DNA or identity: people feel that this is who we are or who we aspire to become.

A POWERFUL FORMULATION

Our experience with framing powerful affirmative topics or core themes has shown us that a thoughtful formulation is important. This entails the following:

- *Positive formulation of the core theme.* It expresses what you want. Our brain cannot think of images associated with the word "not". It will simply skip over the word and form images based on what follows after that word. If you teach a child to cycle and you let go for the first time with the instruction: Careful, there is a pothole. Do not drive into the pothole! Chances are the child will drive into the pothole. More effective is: I am going to let go of you now. Pedal on and keep straight!

- *The affirmative topic indicates what you want more of.* The affirmative topic contains an answer to the questions: Where will we be at the end of the journey? What do we want more of? The wording highlights the wish or aspiration: it contains an indication of the intended direction.

- *Use an unusual combination of words.* In our experience an expression such as "at the speed of light" does not automatically belong to decision-making processes. By intentionally making such an unusual and sometimes paradoxical combination, you positively provoke those with whom you would want to engage in conversation. Metaphors can also be helpful, providing an image that encourages people to associate. The diversity of sensemaking will encourage stakeholders to connect with the theme from their own viewpoint. "Fireworks: using talent to make a bright future", was the theme for a career counselling project. Sometimes, people play with words in such a way that the words carry a double meaning. They indicate where you want to go, and they belong to the context. In a chemical plant the orientation session for new staff members carried the banner: "Chemicals: it's all about connections". In an academic hospital the organizational development project carried the name: "An epidemic of caring".

It is important that the theme touches on the core of what is at stake for the organization or team at that moment. When problems in a specific domain call for attention, it is important that the affirmative topic noticeably links to or builds on that issue. A positive theme that is formulated separately from a tough problem will often be ignored. This is one of the reasons to enter into a dialogue with people to identify what they want and to do the reframing in a dialogue, so that everybody will participate in the mental shift.

AT SCALE – AND IN A GRAIN OF SAND

To see a World in a Grain of Sand
And a Heaven in a Wild Flower,
Hold Infinity in the palm of your hand
And Eternity in an hour.

– William Blake

The choice of the affirmative topic provides direction to the renewal and positive movement forward. There is leadership in this choice. To make the switch from a given problem to a selected theme, is something you could do at a large scale through a major gesture or event, at the beginning of a change process (i.e. some of the examples above). Or you could start this in the common day-to-day situations of every day organizational life. When you realize that your team is tangled up in talking about a problem, then inquire: What would it be like if this problem disappeared? What do we want? Through this you will quickly bring the desired image to the fore and the conversations will shift.

When a colleague is very angry with you about an incident, you can inquire: Why does this situation affect you so much, what is at stake here? Does it go against your sense of fairness or justice or is there another unmet wish or need firing up your emotions? This gives people the opportunity to think of what they really want; which value is important to them. When you have managed to get that out in the open, they know *for what*, rather than *against what* they want to fight (Tjepkema & van Rooij, 2010).

INQUIRING: WITH WHOM?

Creative and sustainable solutions for complex questions will only emerge if there are multiple actors or stakeholders and perspectives involved. The challenge is to bring people with different backgrounds, knowledge, experience and interests together to create a new future. That is not an easy route, because we have designed organizations in such a way (and we have taught ourselves) to split up complexity in controllable fragments.

With an Appreciative Inquiry approach, you try to embrace complexity and play with it. The idea is to use the perspectives of all the stakeholders as much as possible. That makes the question: "Who participates?" a key question at the beginning of each appreciative inquiry. Who is in? Who do we invite into the circle and process of inquiry?

FRAGMENTATION AS OPPOSED TO ACCEPTING COMPLEXITY

Fragmentation or compartmentalization is a strategy to make complexity manageable by separating something big into different smaller fragments or sections. Each of these components can then be addressed separately. The underlying assumption is that it is possible to reconnect the repaired sections and that the whole will function again. This way of thinking belongs to a mechanistic systems view. The assumption in this book is a different one. For us, the starting point is that complexity is a given and is inherently natural, and as a result, cutting up is not possible. If you want to achieve change at the scale of the whole, then fragmentation or compartmentalization is not an effective approach. You need to work in, and with, the whole system.

This implies that as a manager you accept the complexity as a given and organize and cooperate from the underlying differences. Core questions can be: How do we come to new solutions through connecting the differences in a generative manner? How do we find shared sensemaking in different and often opposing interests? What joint challenges can we formulate, so that innovative solutions can be discovered? With AI, the emphasis is on the connection of strengths and the design of settings in which people on the one hand learn to appreciate their differences and on the other hand are able to mobilize the different powers to help construct shared and desired futures.

That is why one of the ground rules of Appreciative Inquiry is that you involve a representation of the whole system, preferably at the same place, in the same moment. What we call: *getting the whole system in the room.* There is an example of a US school for hearing and sight impaired people where not only teaching staff and managers, but also students, and even guide dogs and sign language interpreters participated in an AI summit, because it is so powerful when the whole system is represented and participates.

ALL VOICES IN THE ROOM

The following example shows how the above-mentioned principles can work out. Eddy is the director of a middle school and high school that faces an intense period of change. Currently there are two campuses. Recently, construction started on a new building that will bring all pupils and teachers together in one campus. Moving into this campus is the culmination of a longer process of becoming one school. The current situation is that each campus organizes different types of education; general education, on the one, and technical and professional education on the other. The pupil profiles are quite varied and very few teachers teach on both campuses. Similarly, there are more issues and developments in play at schoolboard level, due to educational policy developments at national government level.

Eddy's core vision for the school is: being a school of warm dialogue. At all levels he initiates, supports and encourages connecting and rich conversations. Based upon this vision the idea emerges for a vision development weekend: a weekend with the purpose to set up a dialogue on the future of the school. The first day focuses on the future vision, the second day on finding the appropriate organizational model.

A leading question during design and preparation is: Who will be invited to this weekend gathering? Who will become co-inquirers of the current strengths of the school and of its vision for the future? Who will learn with whom about the organizational structure? Consistent with the idea of creating a warm dialogue school, a group is formed that mirrors the entire school system, a microcosm of the macrosystem. The result is a group of fifty participants, including pupils, teachers, mentors, secretariat, trade unionists, coordinators, directors, and members of the school board.

The program consists of conversations and interactions in smaller groups combined with plenary exchange sessions. During the first phase, participants identify the key strengths of the school and what positive core they want to take into the future. In the second phase, they dream about the ideal school and share their images amongst each other in a creative manner. The unity in the group is visible. Many people find common ground in what they regard as important for the future of the school.

Next, the groups are asked to formulate criteria that they will use during the second day of the weekend to assess three possible organizational models. The leading question for this is: Which models help us realize our dreams of the future? On day two, three models that were designed in advance are presented and assessed in different groups – using the self-identified criteria. This is quite an exciting step and the implicit question is: Can we keep the same energy that we had on the first day?

From the start of the weekend it was transparent that the school board and group of directors would listen to the participants' assessment of the organizational models and that they, as managing group would take the final decision on which of the models to use to design the schools structure. The big question being: How would this work out? The intention was that during the two days the decision would be made on the structure, to enable the full group of participants to start working on plans to shape this in practice.

As more groups shared their conclusions on the different models, it became clear that everyone's preferences overlapped. Observing this, the chairman of the board stood up and said that there was no need for them to continue to consult with each other separately. With a mix of amazement and pride, he declared the common preference as a formal decision. Following this, everyone could get started on the design question: What was needed to ensure that this decision could become organizational reality? The emerging consensus strengthened and gave confidence for the future, simply because all parties agreed on the set-up.

Working with a broad-based group payed off and when the participants of this two-day vision session were asked what the crucial success factor was, nearly everyone mentioned the presence of the pupils. Not only did they bring an infectious freshness and creative energy to the meeting, they also managed to articulate substantive essence in such a way that it touched others and stirred them. At times this led to amusing spectacles, during which adult groups admitted: "We have come to the same conclusions as the pupils, only they formulated it far more powerfully than we did."

THE ROLE OF THOSE CONCERNED - AND THE KNOWLEDGE NEEDED

Involving stakeholders to learn about and answer questions that are truly relevant for the organization is essential. How then do you select the relevant actors? We found the following questions to be of use:

- For whom is this meant at the end of the day?
- Who should be there if we want to achieve a configuration of the whole – the whole system in the room?
- Who can tell relevant stories about our central theme?
- Who do we need to learn new things about our theme?
- Who will challenge, question and offer constructive critique throughout the dialogues?
- Who might normally not be heard or not have a voice in this issue?

The end users, internal or external (such as clients, pupils, patients), supporters (think of administration, reception, secretariat), and external parties or units with whom you regularly cooperate in the system chain, can easily be overlooked, but these stakeholders do really contribute something when you involve them as co-researcher or co-inquirer. The stream of ideas is richer due to their perspective and through their participation you can develop a sounder sense of group or collective efficacy; a powerful foundation for the implementation of plans.

Such a broad invitation can feel counter-intuitive. This has everything to do with implicit assumptions about what knowledge is needed to take a question forward and your previous experiences with large groups trying to make shared decisions.

In a participatory process on the storage of radio-active waste, scientists were somewhat bewildered that the initiators had also invited civilians. What do they know about radioactive waste? This is such a complex subject, that it is more for specialists and professionals. This remark can be understood from the presumption that you need to work with the right knowledge at the table. In this case: scientifically objective verified data. The underlying thought is that the world around us can be understood objectively: reality can be understood through absolute statements about what is true. It is also the difference between assuming there is an objective, preferred solution, versus an implementable collective action.

Appreciative Inquiry operates from a very different knowledge concept, more from the question: Who has relevant stories (narratives) about this issue? How can we involve the widest possible range of perspectives and knowledge in our search? Can we create a reality with the relevant stories of multiple stakeholders that is most attractive for all of us? In the case of the nuclear waste this was why it was so important to involve citizens. Not to ask them about the appropriate storage measures, because that is not their expertise, rather to hear what their ideas and concerns are around the storage. In this case, it led to an important criterion: Storage may not be indefinite. If over fifty years, an improved storage method is developed, then it should be possible to implement this. This criterion emerged from the care for future generations – their (great) grandchildren.

Relevant knowledge is often located with the end-users of a service or product: students in our schools, clients in our care organizations and customers in shops. One way or another, we sometimes feel uncertain about inviting exactly those people for whom the topic and the inquiry matters most, to contribute to the conversation and the appreciative inquiry. Yet, every time organizations do exactly this, they report that it improves both the relationships as well as the quality of the solutions that emerge.

INNOVATION AS IMPROVISATION

When choosing for Appreciative Inquiry, you know beforehand that you will not be following a detailed plan or designated pathway. You create movement through developing space for stakeholders to take initiatives, to connect, to experiment and to build the bridge as you walk over it. This calls for a combination of the art of allowing things to emerge and to make space for something new, while you resist the temptation of capturing everything that emerges in detail. But it is not laissez-faire either, in the sense that together you search for a direction. Improvisation is a word that describes it well. As Joop Swieringa and Andre Wierdsma (1992) would say: "It's the spirit of the traveler instead of the tourist."

You shape the process one step at a time, responding to what happens and emerges. Such an approach can easily be at odds with the planned-change nature of many other business processes. On occasion you could be lured into drawing up timelines, flowcharts and SMART in between goals. While understandable, this could inadvertently lead to losing the essence (and the strength) of AI. To really apply and hold onto the improvising character (even if at times you are nudged to do it differently) it is important to explore this further. What does improvising mean? What is needed for it to happen?

AN EXAMPLE: PUBLIC SQUARES AS INNOVATION

In their search for new and different approaches, the municipal organization of a large city came up with Public Squares. After having gone through a year-long reorganization process that resulted in a new structure, this Public Squares innovation was intentionally launched. The new arrangements were in place, and the time had come to start working in a different manner: more focus on the city, more collaboration, and an integrated approach to issues and questions.

To offer a platform for the renewal of working methods used within the municipality, the concept of the Public Square was invented: gatherings where all those involved with a "wicked problem" or tough question could gather in order to realize a breakthrough. This approach was a new way of working intended for questions and issues that could not be resolved during regular meetings, for which different parties were needed across departmental borders (sections, managers, regular staff, specialists) and that required creativity. There was a growing, shared experience that existing solutions were no longer working for these issues, they tended to fall off the table or kept on festering. Examples of such issues would be persistent complaints in a neighborhood due to multiple causes, collaboration between different sections of the municipality, or the question of how the municipality could respond differently to innovative initiatives of its residents.

No standard form of meeting, round table, sounding board sessions, or project group was seen as effective for these complex issues. The Public Square image was selected intentionally to imply or connote the image of a village square where people would meet and exchange freely in open and honest conversation. The initiators consciously did not want to specify this any further, as their idea was that they could develop the Public Squares methodology further along the way, together with all stakeholders. They were enthusiastic and keen to inspire colleagues to engage in this new way of working.

Most colleagues responded positively, but it initially proved difficult to invite or attract participants with this metaphor. "What exactly is a Public Square?" was a common question. People wanted a definition, a description of the structure and timeframe. But rather, the initiators responded with a range of different answers: a Square is a good conversation, a Square is an instrument to realize a breakthrough in a tough question, and a Square is a way of setting up a different conversation with and in the city. In this way, they gave answers and at the same time they kept it sufficiently open.

One of the first Squares was about the collaboration between two sections of the municipality who found themselves at odds with each other. One section was responsible for public health and the other for encouraging and facilitating construction projects. The start of these construction projects required a public health ruling to be delivered, often to the irritation of the section responsible for construction. Both sections have a different interest: a healthy city (in relation to clean air for example) versus a city with attractive building projects. The organizers of the Square investigated actively to identify the actual issue and question at stake: What should the Squares topic be? Initially it appeared to be a technical issue on the public health rulings and the process designed for it. Quite quickly it turned out to be about the collaboration and the images both sections had of each other. They therefore chose to co-create a process in which both sections would get to know the respective working worlds of the other. They invited all the staff concerned for a gathering and discovered that this meeting was an intervention in its own right, as most people present had only ever communicated with each other using e-mail.

In small mixed groups, the participants entered in conversations on questions such as: What do you think is important in your work? How is your work organized? The focus was on understanding rather than explaining. Halfway through the day, a participant remarked, "I've come to realize that we use a completely different language".

In parallel, a small group of managers worked on a tough case. During the Public Square, they engaged in a fish bowl conversation, during which participants witnessed the conversation of the managers. Afterwards, the observing participants pointed out a particular moment in which one of the managers had interrupted the conversation to address a number of issues in the conversation, such as the fact that she felt they used different language and needed to take more time to fully understand each other. That intervention made a deep impression on everyone involved. "So that is also possible," was the reaction, followed by: "If she can share her observation to the others, we are allowed to do that as well."

Overall, it was a successful Square in the sense that new forms of collaboration emerged in many ways and this gave a new – generative – impulse to collaborate further in the future. The mutual understanding between sections improved and they managed to connect more easily.

The next Square, on a very different question, had a totally different appearance. No two Squares are the same and that is precisely why this approach is so effective.

HOW TO CONTINUE IMPROVISING? INSPIRATION FROM JAZZ

More and more Squares were organized and experienced as successful. At that time, there was a strong temptation to capture the concept; to formalize it in a road map, a defined method, or best practice. The urge was to make it an institutionalized approach, rather than a metaphor. At the same time, the initiators knew that if they went this route, the Public Square would lose its strength. For no one would explore how they should do a square anymore, but simply implement the road map and consequently lose exactly that what makes it effective. Namely, that people explore together what sort of conversation is needed to achieve a breakthrough: "What should it be about?", "Who should be part of it?", "How do we ensure that this is different from how we normally operate?" and continue to co-create that conversation. Instead, every Square was a different, unique process.

On the basis of the initial experiences, an intermediate solution was developed consisting of seven Public Square principles that explain what a Square is and how you ensure a Square will be effective. On the one hand, this gave more structure to the Public Squares, and thus support for the participants and facilitators. On the other hand, it also carried risks. "We should avoid ending up with a checkmark process. A gathering does not have to meet all principles to be a Square" said one of the initiators. Another said, "These are principles, they are not a checklist." Despite all the unintended temptations from within the organization to reduce the Public Square to a well-defined instrument, the initiators succeeded in making and maintaining space for the playfulness and improvisation of the Squares, and that is exactly what made it successful.

What is needed for this way of working? And why is it so important to make space for improvisation? Jazz music provides enlightening lessons. Besides being a university professor on leadership and organizational development, Frank Barrett is also a talented jazz musician. In his book, *Yes to the Mess* (Barrett, 2012) he describes seven principles from jazz music that help in organizing innovation and change processes:

- The art of unlearning existing routines and patterns: musicians challenge themselves to perform on the edge of their capabilities and because of this, they are not tempted to rehearse a solo prior to the performance or to repeat a performance twice. In organizations, it is inevitable that patterns unconsciously develop that get in the way of learning, change and innovation: This is how it is done around here.

- The capacity to say "Yes to the Mess." As a manager or leader you are often part of situations you did not ask for or that you have no influence on. A productive manner of dealing with these situations is to implicitly say *yes* to everything that comes your way. Do not resist but rather engage with it. It is like improvisational theatre, whatever your counterpart says, you pursue that line of acting. You take it, and move along with it, giving it the direction you think is needed along the way, by shaping your responses.

- Performing and experimenting at the same time. Experimenting helps to make explicit space for mistakes and learn from them. This is a constant process of trial and error.

- Minimal structure, maximum autonomy. Even in jazz, musicians have a minimal structure: a score, an opening riff or chord. Improvising is not possible without this minimal structure. Finding the (organizational) structure that provides just enough stability and security to encourage diversity and innovation is a delicate art.

- Jamming and hanging-out, learning through talking and doing. The equivalent of jamming, are the accidental meetings, conversations and cross fertilizations during work. These do not emerge spontaneously, but they can be encouraged.

- Alternating between taking a solo and backing a performer. As a leader it is sometimes more important to be able to follow and support others to reach good results, then to be in the foreground yourself. Here again we can draw inspiration from the dynamics of a band, in which the members support a soloist in such a way that he/she can shine.

- Develop provocative competence. It is challenging to see the *potential* of a group of people or of a concept, at a moment in which it is not yet really identifiable. Being able to view a situation in two different modes: What is present, now? What is the potential? How can you get there?

It is not coincidental that these principles can all be identified in the example of the Squares. It is remarkable to see that all the stakeholders – from initiator to facilitator to participant – were jointly discovering and learning what Squares are. They were continuously creating and re-creating them together. One could say that they were always learning to Square – a verb instead of a noun. It is a way of doing, thinking and working, rather than a product or fixed form. Above all, it is about engaging in a different type of conversation by focusing on what happens in the undercurrent, asking questions, making unusual combinations of people and taking the time for a reflective conversation.

A conscious choice was made to do the learning and development in-house, rather than engaging external experts to facilitate the Squares. According to the initiators this was the only way to learn – through trial and error and making mistakes. This reflects the principle of simultaneously experimenting and performing. In addition, the form of the Squares is a minimal structure: a loose network of participants, who share a certain way of thinking and viewing the Squares, in such a way that differences are possible and accepted.

The success of the Squares can possibly be attributed to the leadership of the two initiators. At the beginning of the experiment, both explicitly opted for an improvisational approach and maintained this choice or position consciously during the whole process, at times against the dominant vibe. During the first two years of the Squares, they regularly took up the role of guardian for this (new) way of working. They succeeded in this by challenging many stakeholders and by inspiring them to believe that things could be done differently by defining nothing, encouraging a co-creation of working principles, by allowing different images of Squares to exist alongside each other, and especially by ensuring that the Squares could take place.

These behaviors demonstrated several leadership qualities that Barrett identifies as necessary for improvising. For instance, they were very keen to ensure that every Square was different from the last one. Their motto was that Squares were intended to get people out of their groove and to disorientate them. Such a drive requires courage and initiative. Because of their intention to let things emerge, they consciously gave others the space and opportunity to work with the Squares and to develop their own approaches. They also had to be proactive when needed and to provide direction, especially during those moments when the improvisational nature of the Squares was being questioned.

THE ACTION IS IN THE INTERACTION

Although we often speak of organizational change or development, it is actually the people who realize change. Appreciative Inquiry emphasizes this, by approaching organizational development as a social process. In this perspective, change is the result of people having generative conversations and undertaking activities together, from which new initiatives and approaches emerge. The action is in the interaction is a beloved AI expression. Diana Whitney, Amanda Trosten-Bloom and Kae Rader (2010) even identify the core of appreciative leadership as the relational capacity to mobilize creative potential and turn it into positive power. They do not so much point at the leader's ability to enter into new relationships, but rather their capacity to observe, influence, and deepen already existing collaborative relations. For if the relationship works, if people influence each other positively, compare ideas, generate energy and enthusiasm, this will lead to worthwhile outcomes. But how do you achieve that? What should you look for?

CONNECTIONS THAT SPARK ENERGY AND IDEAS

Appreciative Inquiry is a relational practice. All AI interventions have a content and a relational component. They are focused on (a) working on a certain positive theme, and (b) in a specific manner (inquiring, appreciating, together) that influences people's relationships positively. For instance, imagine that you are convinced that the collaboration in your team can be improved, and team members also want to make a next step…

- When framing the affirmative topic for your joint inquiry process, images of the future will emerge from the team members, including what the future means for them *and* motivation to start working on this together will grow.

- During Discovery interviews, the question: When did you truly feel part of a smoothly operating team? will lead to a better understanding of success factors of the team *and* influence the collaboration and mutual trust positively, simply because people share personal stories of each other's and their own strengths-in-action.

- When you embark on an experiment to conduct meetings differently and you try this out for the first time, this gives information on what works in the meetings *and* it strengthens the team spirit.

All of the above only happens if the team members can genuinely inquire together. If a single person dominates in the exploration of the affirmative topic and others are withdrawn, disinterested, cut off, ignored, or otherwise excluded, you will achieve the opposite result. The same applies if the Discovery-interviews are not true conversations in which people really show themselves to each other, but rather dispirited politically correct exchanges of examples or opinions. Or when the experiment or past experience is more evaluated than reflected upon, and judgments prevail over learning. This means that it is essential to pay explicit attention to the quality of conversations and the connections they produce, if AI interventions are to be effective.

In order to get development and learning going as a manager, content aside, it is important to focus on the creation of generative connections between people (Gergen, 2009; Bushe, 2007 & 2013; Zandee, 2013). For example, by formatting the invitation and the conversation in such a way that people feel welcomed and engaged, by framing the questions or agenda items in such a way that chances for connective conversations are maximized and by seizing the opportunity at the beginning of conversations to strike the right, affirmative tone. This holds true for both large and small-scale conversations.

Generative interactions or connections lead to new ideas as well as the energy to work on those ideas. We all have experienced such situations. Some encounters leave you beaming and radiating energy, although at the start of the encounter you were tired, wasted or simply not really switched on. In those cases, something happens, your energy is triggered, and positive emotions come to the fore. You are switched on as if your battery has been charged. Talking is no longer enough; you want to do something! Jane Dutton (2014) researched these types of encounters at work. She called them: *high quality connections*. In some organizations they occur frequently, in others they are quite rare. The beauty of such conversations is that you can create them at any moment. Even colleagues in a team that generally performs poorly, or where people do not know each other very well, can be brought into a high-quality connection. What are the starting points to positively affect the quality of the interaction?

INVOLVE PEOPLE WITH CARE

The way in which people are invited to a conversation, matters. When somebody is invited to a meeting with an obviously thoughtful personal letter or a cheerful invitation, he or she will join the event in a different mode. And when the tone of the invitation is consequently affirmed at the start because the team leader welcomes each participant personally, and explains why everyone is there, the participants feel genuinely included and valued from the onset. Even in smaller conversations and gestures you can convey to people the feeling that they matter, that they are welcome at the gathering, and that you value their voice in the process. In this way, the invitation to people becomes an important undertaking with which you can extend your influence. All this has very pragmatic implications. For instance: what does a first invitation look like? Does someone receive a letter, an e-mail or do you personally call them? How do you phrase the invitation? For what purpose do you invite somebody and how do you phrase this purpose? Why do you specifically value this person's attendance?

During the conversations the same applies; active and attentive listening to what people have to say, drawing them into the conversation and ensuring that they are connected, helps. Body language and posture are important and language also plays a role. Is the latter distant and general or personal and specific? Is the conversational tone directive or inviting, fact-finding or explorative, evaluative or wondering? These factors appear – perhaps unsurprisingly – to play a crucial role and they are worth paying attention to (Dutton, 2014).

When, as a manager, you involve more colleagues simultaneously, you can also have considerable impact on the attention that people pay to each other. Eric, the director of a large hospital initiated a dialogue session with 250 of the 7000 staff members. At the opening, while standing on stage, he stated, "Shortly, we will start the conversations at the tables. When I join in, I am participating as Eric, not as your director. I invite everyone to take your place at the table as yourself, not as your function or your job title". This had enormous impact on the atmosphere of the conversations and the manner in which people listened to each other. Eric's implicit message was: The gathering is not a meeting. This is a conversation that we could also have at the kitchen table, person to person (not role to role), on what concerns us in our hospital.

PLAYFULNESS, HUMOR AND SURPRISE

People who create an event together or have a shared experience develop a bond. A small activity or a surprise turn in a conversation can immediately develop such a mini-experience. We recently conducted performance appraisals with small groups of employees. They were not very keen to do this. At the start of every meeting, we placed a set of picture cards on the table and asked everyone to choose a card that represented their feelings about these conversations. After the initial surprise at the request, meaningful conversations ensued very quickly. People would pick a metaphor or image to express their hopes, their constraints or what the conversations meant for them. Within ten minutes everyone in the circle of participants had spoken and a lot had been said. Even a few jokes had been made. Images can speed things up.

There are lots of variations, of course, to turn a conversation into a joint experience: go for a walk in the woods together to discuss your images of the future, create something together (a movie, collage or flip-over), put the tables to the side in a setting where this is seldom done. The point is that both major and minor interventions can introduce or contribute to playfulness.

INVITATION TO SHARE STORIES

Stories are strong connectors. People who share positive anecdotes around themes that they are concerned about, infect each other. Empathy is triggered, knowledge flows and the energy increases. One person's story is the path to another's future (Whitney, Trosten-Bloom and Rader, 2010). By hearing a colleague talk about something that he or she succeeded in doing, optimism for the future arises along with a sense that that, and more, is possible.

Inviting people to share stories instead of opinions is, therefore, essential. We learned from organizational psychologist, Coert Visser, how the energy in a meeting increases when, at the start, everyone shares a sparkling moment of the past week with his or her neighbor. It can be about anything – as long as the moment was energizing. Within ten minutes the atmosphere in the meeting shifts. People share more stories, as well as statements or facts. In a similar vein, starting with a personal anecdote yourself is very encouraging and can set the tone.

CONFIDENCE IN CAPACITY

Ralph Weickl, an experienced AI facilitator, taught us that it is helpful when a facilitator does not disturb groups in conversation during an AI meeting. This means that you do not walk around to observe and listen (even though the temptation is big). Instead, you let people simply speak together. He would intentionally remain in the front of the space, behind his computer and work on his e-mail, write something – in any case keep himself occupied. With this behavior he did not display disinterest or letting go, he displayed his confidence in the group. People can have great generative conversations. They do not need expert process or meeting facilitation. And it works! Giving confidence is an important accelerator to generate *high-quality connections* (Dutton, 2014).

INVEST IN THE SOCIAL DIMENSION

The last tip is perhaps the simplest one: if AI is a relational practice, then it pays to invest in the social dimension. Give people an opportunity to get to know each other, on a broader level than only exchanging roles or job titles. Often, we tend to let content take the leading role, while it is, in fact, the quality of the interpersonal relationships that leads to breakthroughs.

For example: Edwin, the new director of an engineering plant that faced significant challenges, planned to work on several innovations in the factory, together with the factory operators. For Christmas he and his entire staff with their partners went bowling. This was a party the likes of which they had not seen for years. He didn't really see it as part of the change process, more as something that is nice to do and good for social cohesion in the workplace. Only afterwards did he realize that this get together created a sound foundation for the change process.

Mark, the new director of a school, wanted to organize conversations with a number of teachers whom he knew to have many complaints. Initially, they ignored his invitation – much to his dismay. He didn't really know what to do about it, so he left it at that for a while. Then, during a farewell party of a colleague, he struck up an informal conversation with a few of these teachers about angling, which turned out to be a shared hobby. A week later he received an e-mail message that they were keen to respond to his invitation.

AND MORE IS POSSIBLE

Besides these rules of thumb, the creation of generative dialogue is something that needs to be handled on a case-by-case basis. What is appropriate here? What do we need? Possibly the most important thing is to pay attention, to be aware of the quality of the conversation and relationship. Having a conscious eye for building a collaborative relational space is the central message here. We all have experience with *high-quality connections*. Possibly you can recall some of these for yourself. When were you most energized by a conversation or work interactions? How might this play out for your colleagues and staff members? When are they fully energized in conversation with each other? What happens during such conversations? This reflection will provide you with worthwhile ideas to shape new gestures you can make every day.

The impact of positive emotions that people carry forward following worthwhile encounters cannot be overestimated. Research by people including, Barbara Frederickson, Gretchen Spreitzer and Jane Dutton show positive effects at the individual level (positive emotions support health, vitality and cognitive responses of people), at the team level (confidence, learning from each other, coping with setbacks, commitment) and at the organizational level (organizational effectiveness through better collaboration, coordination and innovation.)

CHANGE HAPPENS ONE CONVERSATION AT A TIME

At times, we work on organizational change during specially designated moments such as an off-site, an extended strategy session, a change meeting or a workshop. Besides these dedicated moments, as a leader or manager you are constantly seeking to encourage change or development in your team, in your (part of the) organization, or in the behavior of a particular team member. The short impulses that you give on the work floor every day are, in the long run, perhaps even more important than the planned, explicit change interventions. Change and movement emerge one conversation at a time. AI works on the principle that conversation is the essence of organizing and, therefore, changing. How can you apply this effectively? And how does it actually work?

DIAGNOSIS AND DIALOGUE

As discussed earlier, Gervase Bushe and Robert Marshak (2014) introduced two perspectives on organizational development: diagnostic and dialogic. In the first perspective, the organization is seen as a machine, for which you in your role as manager, director or consultant, examine what is wrong, as if you were a mechanic and subsequently formulate a diagnosis. The collaboration is poor, the organization is fractured, there is an archipelago of interests, we do not engage in adequate feedback, and so on. Based on this assessment, you present a treatment plan which includes elements like team building sessions away from the office, a conversation with that one defiant team member, or improvement project groups. These can then be planned and scheduled. The underlying assumptions are that something in the system is broken which needs to be fixed, and that a specific movement can be started based on well-chosen interventions (*unfreeze-move-refreeze.*) In this perspective, change is seen as the exception to the rule and as a temporary situation intended to resolve a particular problem or to overcome a gap or deficit.

The second perspective, dialogic organizational development, sees change or rather, development, as ongoing, continuous. The organization is a self-organizing and socially constructed living system; a process of organizing that evolves continuously and is shaped every day by the sum total of all the stories and conversations happening between people. Organizing is the consequence of sensemaking and decisions that occur in dialogues – nothing more and nothing less. The role of a change agent or leader is to help shape those dialogues, or conversational spaces, to be as collaborative and generative as possible.

YOU CAN LIVE A GOOD STRATEGY

Take for example the story of a manager of an educational institution who wanted to work on strengthening the connections between teachers, management, the staff departments and school board. The groups were clearly quite distant from each other and there was even distrust. The school was in the process of implementing significant innovations and many teachers didn't feel involved or willing to participate.

To strengthen teachers' participation and increase feelings of connectedness and a sense of belonging, the manager planned a number of interventions which she included in her year plan, such as coffee table conversations, a newsletter, workshops, team off-sites. She also had a very practical and personal aspiration based on the motto: you can live a good strategy. If a teacher approached her with a plan, a complaint, an informative question, a proposal, or a request, she would reply that same day. Regardless of the number of unanswered messages in her inbox and missed calls, teachers *always* received a reply the same day, even if it was only an acknowledgement or thank you message. In this manner the manager created minor meaningful connections on a daily basis – both for the teachers and for herself.

After a year, something appeared to have shifted. Teachers had the feeling that they were seen and taken seriously in the school. The intentional large change interventions had, undoubtedly, contributed to this – but the countless individual, short conversations and emails with the teachers had fed this just as much. In any case, they were mentioned surprisingly often during the conversations at her farewell party and on the goodbye cards she received.

ORGANIZING CONVERSATIONS

The essence is that change happens through conversing rather than conversing *about* the change. You enact or *are* the change that you want to see. Naturally, as a manager you do not have to be the (only) change agent all the time. It is not about your conversations only. You can also organize conversations between people. For instance, if the aim is to improve client focus, you can organize a series of conversations in which people discuss relevant issues for clients together. Preferably on the basis of a question that encourages connection through story sharing *and* triggers people to display client focus immediately, just by answering the question.

For example: the Board of Directors of an accountancy firm were very keen that while reporting, their auditors would argue more from the perspective of their clients – and not only from their own professional background or from the legal and regulatory frameworks. To this end, they organized a series of summer client interviews on the question: What energizes our clients? What issues do our clients face? Accountants ventured out, collecting information on the issues that clients faced and analyzed and exchanged their findings together. The directors were present during these meetings, not to facilitate them, but rather to think along with the auditors, using their own accountancy experience. This generated a lot of energy and ideas on how to make the reports more client-focused. Rather than telling the accountants to become more client-focused, the directors had asked them a question that automatically shifted their perspective and helped the whole group become more client-oriented.

Similarly, a large municipality was very keen to ensure that its social policies were more centered on what the citizens experienced. They organized a series of discussion evenings during which civil servants entered into conversation with different groups and stakeholders in the city on what they were proud of and what they worried about. Every conversation ended with the question: With whom would you want to continue the conversation on this theme? This triggered a chain reaction that made it obvious to everyone internally and externally that the municipality wanted to do things differently. It did not lead to a new policy plan, but rather the conversations in and of themselves invited the civil servants to work in a different and more participatory way, and to center citizen's experiences within the framework of their current policy plans.

A CONVERSATION AS AN EXPERIENCE: THE
IMPORTANCE OF MICRO-MOVES

Organizational learning scholar, Nancy Dixon, explains this phenomenon as: organizational change happens one conversation at a time. This suggests that the very next conversation is a new opportunity to influence the future. Change is no more than a string of conversations, small and large. Patricia Shaw (2002) takes this idea even further by stating that conversing is identical to organizing. Having a conversation, according to her, is not just a method for organizational change; *it is* organizing and changing, at the same time.

Jeff is a manager who, because of his role, was responsible for conceptualizing and implementing a new system for knowledge sharing in his organization. He experienced this as a very demanding process and although he realized that things had started to move, he was puzzled and could not grasp how and why this happened. At his request, we reconstructed the change process with him and made an overview of the crucial moments that had led to a breakthrough. His story illustrates the impact of conversations that are an experience of change.

The process of building a knowledge management system for Jeff's company kicked off with a series of formal sessions involving stakeholders from the entire organization. After a couple of months, in which a considerable amount of time and energy was devoted to analyzing key questions and objectives, thinking through the design specifications for a knowledge management system, and producing a 200 (!) page report, there were many concerns. Would the new system perform? What would the price tag be? What would it look like? Which knowledge would it capture and which not? How do you ensure that people really start using it? In short, the process was stuck.

The turning point occurred during a telephone conversation with Jeff and his manager, who asked him a very simple question: After three months of hard work, can you tell me about a concrete and tangible result that boosted your energy? This was a radically different question than the questions the team had been working on. Jeff couldn't come up with an answer and realized after a long silence that he really had to approach this in a totally different way. Subsequently he invited four colleagues with whom he liked to work to discuss the process. In no time, they came up with a totally different set-up, a design that, as its starting point, inquired into the process of knowledge sharing and activating colleagues, not on how a new system needed to be built. The system became a means to an end, not the aim. The idea fit on two pages. With that they presented their plan to the board, which immediately allocated them the necessary budget needed to realize the new system.

All sorts of conversations in this process potentially could have led to the revitalizing of the process. It could have been any of the formal design sessions, conversations with Jeff's managers, board meetings, workshops with external advisors, project group meetings, etc. However, Jeff identifies that particular conversation with his manager as the breakthrough moment. He sees this as the conversation in which the change, the new approach that would lead to a breakthrough, became visible in a miniature version. In this conversation, Jeff began to think differently about his way of working. Triggered by the one question of his manager: Have you created anything that gives you energy? He felt both the energy – and the lack thereof – immediately. It was a conversation about the new approach and, at the same time, a mini-experience of it.

Karen Golden-Biddle (2014) calls such moments, *micro-moves*. We have all experienced micro-moves and their effects. Those interactions that foster disengagement, inciting disbelief that change will happen, and by contrast, those interactions that facilitate engagement, inciting a collective sense of hope that one's effort will make a difference in achieving change. A generative conversation, a conversation that in itself contributes to a personal sense of movement, awakening or insight, is typically not a conversation during which you talk about change, but wherein you experience the change itself, or the new future.

WHO BEGINS? ACTION AND REACTION

How can you recognize and use these types of moments? Can you create your own micro-moves, even outside the planned conversations? It sounds somewhat abstract, but it helps to see all conversations as a sequence of *gestures and responses*, as the American sociologist and philosopher George Herbert Mead (1863 – 1931) articulated it.

You do not always have to initiate this yourself. You can also respond to somebody who makes a gesture or puts out an invitation in the form of a question or an observation. Your response can be anything, from talking enthusiastically about an idea to leaving the conversation in anger, from saying nothing to asking a question, from sharing how this makes you feel to presenting a different viewpoint. Whatever you do, the gesture of the initiator only becomes meaningful through your response. This, of course, also holds in the opposite; your gestures only get their meaning through the responses of others.

An example from daily life illustrates this. Two children of one of our colleagues regularly had arguments. Whenever our colleague addressed them, they would both shout: But he/she started it! As if the responsibility for the fights *only* belonged to the one who started it. Following a new row between his kids, our colleague, in an effort to find a different entry point to shift the situation, started an inquiry with them. What happens when you are having a fight? You say that the one who started the row is the cause of it, but is this true? Could it be that a fight occurs not due to the one who started it, but by the way the other one responds to it? He used the fresh incident when the son had made a negative remark about his sister's outfit, whereupon she snapped back, and a row ensued. Together they playfully explored alternative responses. "What else could you have said as a response to the remark about your dress?" our colleague asked. Instantly, three alternatives were pitched, including, "OK, so your taste is different to mine." Whereupon our colleague asked his son, "How would you have responded, if she had said that?" His son shrugged his shoulders, "Well... in that case I would have let it go. There would be no fun in going on." In all its simplicity, this is an empathic example. Even if the other person opens the dance, your reaction influences the dynamics of a conversation just as much. What choice do you make?

Besides carefully choosing your reactions and responses you can also explicitly assess the gestures that you see as inviting and consistent with the development that you want to realize. When you are keen on more connectivity, you could, for instance specifically ask members in a team meeting for their input. If you are interested in shifting to thinking from the outside in, then you can use that as your anchor and regularly ask, "Do we know what the client thinks about this?" With that question you pre-empt the emphasis needed. The difficulty is of course, that you can only control your own gesture, and not the response of the other. Certain gestures evoke specific responses, but there are no guarantees. However, it remains valuable to reflect on your choices and never assume that because your gesture came from a certain role or position that it is understood as you intended. It is vital to listen for and to understand the various responses. This can make the difference between an ordinary moment and a micro-moment with which you contribute to the sought-after development.

Which gestures are inviting or accelerating and which reactions are helpful cannot be identified in general. Everything depends on the theme of the desired change. The question is: What works to create an experience that reflects the desired future now – even if it is only in this one moment? If you, for instance, want to increase employee involvement, then the dialogue that initiates the change program needs to model engaged and involved employees. The opening gestures need to mimic the larger future desired state. Managers, who adopt this perspective, see small opportunities every day. Some you can predict and plan and others occur spontaneously.

PAYING ATTENTION TO THE DARK SIDE

A question that often pops up is how AI deals with negativity. Is the idea that you only talk about what is going well or what succeeds? Or could you also have an eye for the frustrations, fears and anger in an organization? The latter is definitely the case. Even more so, attempting to avoid negative feelings or neglecting them is counterproductive. Earlier, in the chapter, "From Problem Given to Chosen Topic", we discussed how it is possible to search for the affirmative topic or the unmet wish underneath a problem. It's even possible to take a step further and use AI as an unexpected perspective to make something painful discussable. That can be very powerful. The question is how to go about it.

THE PITFALL OF POSITIVE QUESTIONS

In the Discovery phase, an appreciative inquiry typically begins with questions about past successful experiences – creating a focus on life-giving forces and strengths. Participants question each other on inspirational experiences and stories about highlights related to the core theme of the inquiry. The idea is to learn from factors that have made these successes possible up to now. Regardless if these experiences are rare or commonplace, the invitation is to give attention to those moments when something did succeed. For example, with a group that wanted to know more about powerful collaboration we used the following question: Tell me about a moment in which you were a member of a group that managed to achieve a great result through powerful collaboration, an outcome that you would never have been able to realize on your own, where the constellation of people was essential for the success. What is the story that immediately comes to mind?

In some cases, this approach does not work. Gervase Bushe (2011) even calls this a pitfall. Sometimes, positivity can implicitly start to dominate in such a way that a form of censorship emerges in the AI processes. People get the sense that they are not allowed to express criticism and concerns, or that there is no space for negative experiences. This is amplified if facilitators or managers underline that it is time to focus on successes and positivity. We emphasized earlier that the core of AI is not about being positive, rather it is its *generative nature*. Positivity can support this, but it is not always sufficient.

It can become counter-productive if people get the feeling that they *have* to talk about something positive, even though their energy is centered on things that bother or worry them. In that case, the positive question will end up triggering a conversation beside the theme rather than about the theme, and the essential connection will not happen.

An illustration: During a reorganization of a large administrative company a group of middle managers were caught in a bind between the Board and employees on the work floor. They wanted to be loyal to the Board, but often struggled to present the vision and plans with the necessary zest to their staff members, as they were not always in full agreement. In a similar vein they struggled to channel the resistance and criticism of staff to the upper echelons. This position demanded a lot of energy and at times would give them the feeling that they could never do it right. This became very obvious during an afternoon that was supposed to be about the change process. Nobody could summon the energy to discuss the issue openly, but it was very noticeable in the general atmosphere. It was obvious that exploring the change as if everything was going according to plan would not be a sensible move. We cancelled the program and instead invited the managers to talk in fours about themselves and about how they managed to uphold themselves in this tight spot they found themselves in – stuck between the top and the work floor, especially on the occasions that they felt they could not make a good contribution in anybody's eyes. How did they handle this? How did they do cope with it as well as possible? There were many examples of such moments, only these had never been explored. Sharing and unravelling these moments gave a lot of insight and increased self-confidence. This made a significant contribution as this issue was of major concern for this group.

NO LIGHT WITHOUT SHADOW: HOW TO TAKE THE NEGATIVE SIDE ALONG?

One way of dealing with the question on how positive AI needs to be is not to think in terms of positive-negative. Both sides are inseparably connected with each other. There is no low tide without high tide, no day without night, no light without shadow, no happiness without unhappiness. As Carl Jung describes, I would rather be whole than good. The main point is: what type of inquiry does justice to the situation and allows discoveries to be made from inside that situation? In other words, how can the pain or negativity be recognized, while at the same time seeds of hope are uncovered by the way in which the dark side is discussed?

An example: In an AI learning network that we organized for a group of eighty participants, the following question emerged repeatedly: What do you do with AI in turbulent times? We decided to arrange an experience for this question as we found that merely talking about it didn't lead to new ideas. We invited participants to interview each other in pairs. The introduction was: Every person or organization enters into situations or periods that are truly problematic or tough, such as moments of misfortune, pain or even suffering. Subsequently participants asked each other: Tell me a personal story that illustrates such a moment or period that was stressful, possibly even tragic and that stays with you as a difficult time and from which you have managed to grow in one way or another? The participants were invited to use the following questions to inquire further into the stories:

- What kept you upright during this period? What kept you standing?

- What carried you forward, how did you find the strength to continue?

- What gave you energy and courage?

- Looking back at this story, maybe you came out of it stronger. What did you discover about yourself? What strengths have you uncovered?

After the conversations in pairs, participants exchanged their discoveries in small groups and made meaning out of it. Finally, each group noted conclusions by completing one or more of the following sentences:

- People regain confidence or develop resilience if …

- People draw courage from difficult periods when …

- People succeed in finding hope and possibilities in difficult periods when …

- People and organizations manage to develop themselves in difficult periods if they…

- Tragedy, loss and suffering become meaningful if …

These sentences were displayed in the room and read aloud. The intimacy and respect in the group was overwhelming, as if an essential understanding connected the participants. The question on possibilities of AI in turbulent times vanished into thin air. The sentences spoke for themselves.

EXAMPLES OF POWERFUL QUESTIONS

Some more examples of powerful questions that we have used in AI trajectories....

- *Theme: Care in a Hospital*

Question: The nature and conditions of our work entail that you often need others to provide good care and services. Especially at those moments that are challenging or demanding, you experience that it is crucial to care for each other. Feeling supported by others makes you push through, even in tough situations. Can you tell me a story of when you felt supported by a colleague (or colleagues) at a moment when you really needed it? I am also curious about when you showed your care for a colleague in need. Could you give me an example, please?

- *Theme: Uncertainty in an Innovative Setting*

Question: Can you tell me a story of when uncertainty brought you to a result that would not have been possible without that uncertainty – a story in which uncertainty was a condition for what emerged?

- *Theme: Dealing with Mistakes*

Question: We work in a setting in which making mistakes is inevitable. The way in which we respond to errors is more important than the illusion that we could avoid these errors. If you look back, is there an example of a moment when it went wrong well? Meaning that we were able to respond adequately and to genuinely learn from this incident?

DRAWING STRENGTH FROM THE NEGATIVE

The above illustrates that an inquiry from an appreciative perspective does not necessarily imply that negative experiences are ignored or evaded. On the contrary, discussing and exploring such experiences can lead to very rich conversations. What is helpful is to approach them from the standpoint of their potential, from the perspective of hopefulness rather than helplessness. As a result, people involved feel seen and recognized in their emotions. Using an inquiry approach, the experience is questioned step by step. This gives a fresh perspective and renewed strength. AI means inquiring into what is to be valued in, or from, an experience. It is not about choosing between either positive or negative.

CONDUCTING AN ORCHESTRA

How do you lead a process of Appreciative Inquiry? Or rather, how do you support it, give it direction and ensure that it continues? Compared to the more planned change processes with detailed planning and activity overviews, AI is a process focused, rather than a project focused way of working.

Frequently leaders, who embark on working with AI, reflect that letting go is their biggest challenge. I need to be less directive and in control and become better at letting go, was the conclusion of one manager we worked with. We inquired further: You know precisely what you want to do *less* of. Can you also tell us what you would want to do *more* of? Can you describe what it looks like if you let go? A lively discussion ensued during which the metaphor of the conductor emerged. In the following section, we will explore this. Firstly, we start with a short exploration of the question of why typical managing is not the most suitable leadership style if you want to evoke positive change.

WHY NOT MANAGE?

The *Handbook of Positive Organizational Scholarship* discusses two paradigms: the management paradigm and the development paradigm. Organizations are generally constructed on the (often implicit) perspective of a management paradigm where there is a predictable task that is divided amongst colleagues and functions or departments. SMART formulated targets provide a smart structure and labor division to ensure efficiency and swift execution of work. By closely monitoring progress with targeted KPIs it is possible to adjust when necessary. This paradigm and approach is useful in cases characterized by efficiency focus and predictability of tasks. A different perspective is to look at an organization as a group of people who jointly want to realize a specific purpose by conversing, performing, experimenting and building the bridge as they walk upon it. This is what the handbook calls the development paradigm. This latter approach is more about creating direction, supporting and enabling, than about prescribed aims and tight control. In any organization there is an inevitable tension related to these two paradigms. We explored this in-depth in the first chapter of this book.

A common pitfall in the practice of AI – which is completely grounded in the development paradigm – is using the management and control paradigm to conduct AI. Creating movement and development according to the AI philosophy is a fundamentally different approach than managing change. But what sometimes happens is that we copy daily habits and organizational practices and then apply these in the micro-cosmos of the change process, though the idea behind AI as a philosophy of change is to engage in a new or different way, in an inquiry mode, instead of in an efficient production mode. Innovation groups often are affected by the contagion of the managerial patterns. The aim of a working group outside the departmental structure is to create an alternative setting, where *out of the box* thinking and innovating is possible, and where existing functions and hierarchy are irrelevant. But it is all too easy for the working group to find itself in a traditional meeting arrangement, with formal minute taking, prescriptive planning, and members implicitly expecting the manager to take decisions after the brainstorm. This may appear as a sound logical and comfortable approach but unfortunately it is inconsistent with the process of AI, and thus undermines it.

Ikujiro Nonaka (Nonaka & Takeuchi, 1995), in an analogy of the Windows Program, introduced the metaphor of the software program Windows to an organization. Can we look at an organization as having multiple layers, like a computer has multiple windows? Each has their own rules and meaning, and in each you perform different functions. Can you switch between windows and operate in separated realms that have their own set of rules? Can you one day be a manager who conducts a quarterly progress meeting with your superior on the results of your department and the following day take a very different role and work according to a different set of rules in your change process? And which rules might those be? What type of role is appropriate? It is definitely more than just letting go…

THE SILENT CONDUCTOR

In his book *The Art of Possibility* the famous American conductor Benjamin Zander writes about his exploration of being a conductor of an orchestra. An important experience for him was the moment he realized that he felt overly responsible for the music and performance. Over time, in his mind it had become *his* job, even though he knew he was the only member of the orchestra who did not play an instrument. A conductor stays quiet but does play a key role. He moved his focus from the *task* (making music) to the people (the musicians). He decided: my role is to ensure that collectively they choose to do their best, give all that they've got so that a great musical performance emerges (Zander & Zander, 2002). This insight changed his focus. For instance, he began to explore how he could learn whether the orchestra members were in good spirits. Did they perceive that they could make a significant contribution or not? How could he discern their state of being? He tried reading it from their faces, sometimes he asked, but he remained in doubt.

One day he decided to experiment with *blank sheets*. On every music stand he placed a blank sheet of paper. He invited the orchestra members to note feedback, thoughts and tips at the end of the rehearsal. Did they agree with his interpretation of the piece, the tempo, and the emphases he made? Did they have any further ideas for improvements? In the beginning the musicians needed to get used to this approach. As time progressed, more sheets were handed in and Zander received increasingly useful input. In an orchestra of a hundred people, there are always musicians who envision the composition differently than others, or who have an idea on how their section could sound even better and thus improve the quality of the performance.

The blank sheets are a simple intervention, permitting a whole new dynamic to develop between the conductor and the orchestra. The conductor, the leader, became an *inquirer*, very visibly on a quest for the most appealing interpretation of the composition, instead of the person who knows and directs how the composition should be played. The responsibility for an appealing performance was now everyone's responsibility. Every member felt that he or she could make a useful and essential contribution. This shows how small, but significant interventions, based on an inquiring mindset can have far reaching results.

A DESIGN MINDSET

Frank Barrett's (2012) view on leadership goes even further. The management and control paradigm discussed above depends on managers taking a role as a decision maker who trusts rationality, gap analysis and who leads planning sessions to minimize risks and correct errors. Barrett has a very different perspective of the leader in an appreciative inquiry. In his view, leaders in such a role should adopt a design mindset. Leadership in a design activity means creating space, sufficient support and challenge so that people will be challenged and invited to grow by themselves. The leader becomes someone who encourages, but also organizes and dis-organizes, creates space and provides direction by asking provocative and stimulating questions. Someone who looks at the people and the way they think and act, and asks himself: Are they curious and still growing or does the conversation threaten to unwind to a non-constructive, routine exchange? Can/should I do something to fan the process? There is no fear of letting go of control because, as we discussed, control is an illusion. Tracking, fanning, and inviting are better words to describe this type of leadership behavior.

HOW DO YOU DO THAT?

At the World AI conference 2012, Gervase Bushe and Ronald Fry gave a keynote speech on how to make the most of AI processes. This talk was based on their review of a large number of AI-interventions. Their research showed that the most successful development processes (in the sense that they are transformative) have something in common in the way they are managed or supported. The leaders in those processes adhere firmly to the development paradigm, the dialogical approach to change and their underlying principles.

Bushe and Fry explain with an example: In the dream-phase, when people are invited to share and exchange images of a desired future, it is very helpful *not* to summarize or arrange them. Fill the entire space with all kinds of images. Do not place them in some sort of order, do not try to focus on one specifically or identify the so-called most shared ideal image. Let the images be images. People do not have to see them all… Sometimes it is better to just look at the artefacts in small groups. You do not need an overview; our brain is not capable of grasping the richness of a large sum of images all at once. The importance and the power of dreams, in the form of posters, drawings, collages or whatever, is that they have been made, says Fry. The materialization of our imagination is an important step in transforming our intentions into actions. There is no need to summarize or to come to one preferred image.

When it comes to experimentation, space for improvisation is essential, Fry explains. Generative design implies that we make our hopes and dreams visible, as a first step towards action. The most important feature is not that we talk about our intentions or produce action plans, but that we start co-creating something immediately, even if it is nothing more than a very rough prototype. The key to a powerful Design phase in AI is that people really come on board as if they are real owners of the ideas and change actions to come. If all goes well, faith and courage have been built in the previous phases, but the step to action calls for a *leap of faith* and *courage*. Stakeholders literally dive in, start playing and try things out together. This is not about how good or effective the prototypes are. As a manager or facilitator, you are not worried about that. Rather, your main attention is focused on: are people engaged, are they active, and are they exhibiting a sense of purpose and ownership?

Fry strongly argues for embracing mistakes and errors, much like Barrett saying "Yes to the Mess." Making space for this is something you can really do as a manager. Fry shares the story of a design agency with a *wall showcase of mistakes*, failed prototypes, in their office. It is very obvious as it is one of the first things that meet the eye upon entering. They are not afraid, and do not hide their mistakes. On the contrary, they value and embrace them, as these were necessary and essential to later success. We need to find ways to allow mistakes to be present as openings or opportunities for true innovation.

In the moment of moving from ideas and intentions to concrete actions and experiments, a further focal point becomes important. Here, you might end up turning the *emergent process into a project*. For example, because one person starts documenting all ideas, or writes an action plan in order to allow for progress monitoring, the implicit assumption is that behavior will follow: people will actually do what is written down. However, if real ownership and accountability has not yet been established, this works counterproductively. Don't "project-ize" too quickly, warn Bushe and Fry. That is the most expedient way to unintentionally remove ownership from people. What really works, according to Bushe, is to assist people to take the first step *themselves;* a voluntary, visible action and follow that movement attentively, by staying close to that energy. Observe closely what happens and if beautiful things begin to emerge, shine a light on those and look for ways to make them even brighter, stronger or bigger. This requires improvisation. Bushe compares the role of managers and leaders in this phase with that of a gardener; the seeds have been sown, now is the time to wait and observe. Fertilize the plants that you want to see grow, weed when needed…. Especially in hierarchical organizations, managers can find this refreshing. You do not have to monitor every detail and correct swiftly, nor do you have to push unmoving ideas and images along for too long. The improvisational, emergent, and self-managing energy is contagious. People simply need to know the leader is interested in their progress, learning and contribution.

How essential this is, became apparent to us when working with a team that sought to work on their own development and designed an AI process for that purpose. Their desire was to collaborate more and to become more united. This started with two actions; coining a team action-plan and organizing Friday afternoon get-togethers. The team plan was realized swiftly and then, to everybody's surprise, the informal Friday afternoon sessions failed... Initially everybody supported the idea enthusiastically, but after two months the gatherings had hardly been attended. The initiators wanted to give up, as they were disappointed in their colleagues and feared they had failed. The initiative that was intended to encourage connectivity and to emphasize the possibility of having more influence was on the brink of collapse. Fortunately, during a team meeting, the manager succeeded in starting a true inquiry far beyond a mere evaluation of the Friday afternoon attendance. "We all thought this was a good plan, nevertheless, the turnout is disappointing. What is happening? Do you still support the idea?" Everybody confirmed that the energy was still there. "What is needed to make it happen?" became the leading question, instead of inquiring: why aren't you coming? The team suggested attempting a different day, earlier in the week. Thus, Friday afternoon drinks became Thursday lunch meetings. The framing that the action had not failed and that as a team they could explore options that would possibly work better, was as important for the development of the group as the actual lunches themselves.

As basic approaches to leadership, managing and orchestrating possess their own logic and their own value. For an AI process, the fundamental assumptions of AI are best served by orchestration. There is nothing as de-energizing or demoralizing for participants in a participatory process like AI than management taking on the ideas of people for actions as recommendations. The challenge for the leader in AI is creating an environment that allows for ideas to emerge *and* mobilizes that same generative energy to realize the proposed ideas.

INTERVIEW: ERWIN DE BRUYN - STEBO

FINDING GOOD SOLUTIONS FOR SOCIAL CHALLENGES, THAT'S WHAT DRIVES ME AND OUR ORGANIZATION.

Erwin De bruyn is the director of Stebo, a social profit organization based in Genk. This organization originated from social engagement following the closure of the coal mines in the province of Limburg. At the beginning, the emphasis was on neighborhood and community work, later on, Stebo went through a major development and growth process. Currently its focus includes several issues: housing, work, entrepreneurship and energy. The organization was pivotal in undertaking several initiatives that since their start-up have become part of, and anchored in, Flemish government policies.

PRINCIPLES, NOT JUST A METHOD

Thinking of Appreciative Inquiry, I make a distinction between the methodological side and the principles and foundations. The method is interesting in its own right as it empowers you with practical tools and helps you design processes. But my experience is that if you focus merely on the methodological side, this leads to a type of fatigue in the organization: "Oh no, yet another exchange in pairs about a success experience." However, if you start from principles, then you have an endless number of methodological variations. For us, this works within the organization, when formulating targets, forming teams, and organizing work. In the outside world, it is also the basic approach we adopt when working on social change.

AUTHENTIC DIALOGUE WITH MULTIPLE PERSPECTIVES

The essence of Appreciative Inquiry for me is authentic dialogue. It starts with a deep respect for what others are and do. That is the appreciative part of it. To that you add the element of inquiry; the genuine understanding of where the other is. In this way you can bring the multiple perspectives together. I make an effort to avoid entering a relationship based on my self-righteousness and opt for modesty instead; there are always multiple perspectives. If you recognize and acknowledge that, you can contribute your own perspective, without rigidly having to hold onto it. It is about looking for a combination of being aware of your strengths and being humble at the same time. That grounded attitude is what we seek to express as an organization too, making us an attractive party for others. We understand that multi-actor collaboration is always about working with multiple perspectives. There is, and has to be, room for every-body. Successes are shared and when we suffer a setback, we also share that responsibility together.

An example: we advise local authorities on how to develop their housing poli-cies. We have completely opened up the consultations on this by organizing broad stakeholder meetings. Everyone who has a stake in housing in a specific municipality gets a place at the table. Policy makers initially felt considerable anxiety over this approach, especially as we were not providing them with the director's role that they were used to. For us, an important principle was that the municipal authorities are just one voice in the multitude of voices. We felt it was essential to improve the quality of the dialogue through carefully design-ing the questions with which we started the conversation. This is an example of the methodological side of Appreciative Inquiry that we have mastered, and it worked. In hindsight the municipal authorities admitted: "For us this was not an easy route, but we are astounded by the richness of the insights that have emerged".

HOW WE TALK ABOUT THINGS. AND: WHAT WE TALK ABOUT (AND WHAT WE DON'T.)

What helps me in these contexts is what I learned from the philosopher Wittgenstein: *The borders of my language are the borders of my world.* The realization that reality is a language game and a choice rather than a given fact, makes you so much more flexible. That is what fascinates me: by taking a meta-position, you can observe the language in which the others are caught up. I love to mull that over. Not by positioning myself outside or above the game, but rather from participating actively in the conversation. This may sound abstract, but I might do this by describing what is happening and then re-formulating that as a question, or by asking a question about something that feels as if it is not allowed or not supposed to be investigated. That sometimes take courage, as you cannot control how others will look at you. It is easier to choose for the relative safety of playing the game as it is and adhere to dominant consensus. But I enjoy breaking the conversation open so that we discuss what truly needs to be discussed. I call things by their name, just because I want to be involved and work with others to establish something.

KEEP LOOKING FOR POSSIBILITIES

As a managing director, AI inspires me every day to keep looking for possibilities. During recent years, we have felt the impact of the economic crisis in our country; valuable social initiatives came under increased scrutiny by the government. However, being angry about this does not help. The art is to ask myself every morning: "Where do I see opportunities, movement? What are we willing to let go of? Where could we be more pragmatic?" There are many different ways of doing the right thing, and that is why I have little trouble of letting go of something that we were doing well. For me my compass is clear; my journey in life is about finding effective solutions for social challenges. That is what drives me and drives Stebo as well. We aim for that combination of sound business operations and working with social challenges.

BUILDING BLOCKS: QUESTIONS, CONVERSATIONS, STORIES, ACTION

QUESTIONS THAT PROVIDE DIRECTION

To initiate a change process, it is possible to start with an answer, an idea or a plan. But it is not absolutely necessary. In AI, we use questions as a vantage point. Questions create space for learning, for creativity and for new ways of thinking (Vogt, 2003). We work from the assumption that the question determines the direction in which a system develops. There are no neutral questions; whatever you focus on is amplified. A problem-oriented question can be perfectly appropriate in some contexts, but it does not always set the direction for new solutions.

In this chapter, we will explore this notion of starting from questions. How do you choose a question that triggers people to inquire? With which question do you direct attention towards the most productive qualities of a team or organization? What question enables the people involved to access that which gives life to them and their organization?

THE UNCONDITIONAL POSITIVE QUESTION

The question at the heart of an Appreciative Inquiry is always an unconditional positive question (Ludema, Cooperrider and Barrett, 2001). It starts from capacity and drive and awakens the positive core of a group or system:

- When are we at our best? What contributes to that? What is the DNA of our system that enables us to grow and develop?

- How can we build on those qualities and strengthen them in the future?

This positive core question creates energy, strengthens connections and invites new ideas. Fry and Barrett (2005) describe an experiment in which they invited two groups of people from the same organization to ask two different sets of questions to their colleagues. One group went to work with a question based on an Appreciative Inquiry perspective and the other with a topic that was formulated from a problem-focused, analytical perspective. Both groups were unaware of the other. When presenting the research findings, the results were totally different; the first group had examples of a vibrant organization with motivated staff, while the second presented a list of fifty problems and questioned the opportunities for survival of the organization itself. Besides that, the first group was very keen to get going again and had also managed to trigger the energy of their respondents, simply by conducting their interviews. By contrast, the second group had become totally dispirited and was pessimistic about the opportunities for the organization to revive itself. In short, this story illustrates the enormous impact of the direction of a question: both on the findings and also on the energy of people to engage with a theme or issue.

CRAFTING QUESTIONS

So, does this mean we always have to ask the exact same question? The short answer is no... It's not as simple as that. There are many possible variations of a positive question. The point is to search for and formulate the question that will create energy at that moment in time with the people in that particular system. The crafting and fine-tuning of the question is an important activity in the design of an Appreciative Inquiry. The first thing to explore is: which question creates the desired effect? Which question has the possibility to evoke a conversation that moves us a step forward, together?

There is a famous anecdote about how David Cooperrider spent three months crafting a single question. His challenge was to formulate the opening question for a conversation amongst religious leaders from around the world. He finally decided upon: Can you tell me about the moment in which you knew you wanted to live your life in service of religion? This is a variation of the first positive question we mentioned above: the question asks for people's principle and deepest motivation and goal. Typical for an Appreciative Inquiry process is that Cooperrider did not ask this question himself to the people involved, but instead invited people to enter into a conversation with each other led by this question. The craftsmanship of an Appreciative Inquiry practitioner lies in thinking upfront about questions that have the possibility to set something in motion – and to invite the people that are touched by that question to use it for an inquiring dialogue.

In this context, Gervase Bushe (2013) talks about generative questions; questions that you expect to have an effect, and that you design specifically to be as impactful as possible. He proposes that a generative question typically:

- creates a connection between the people who are in conversation about it
- is surprising
- touches the head as well as the heart
- (has the potential to) create a shift in thinking or a change of perspective

All of these qualities can be found in Cooperrider's opening question. With these principles in mind it is possible to start crafting your own generative questions, which is often easier said than done... It does not always take three months to formulate the right question, but it does happen regularly that we spend a few days thinking about a question and revise it several times. Adding, replacing, or subtracting a word can totally alter the question and cause a different effect. And different people react differently to the same word. So, it might help to try the question on a number of people and to experience the effects. Based on the feedback, you can refine the question and ask it again.

THE ARCHITECTURE OF POWERFUL QUESTIONS

Vogt, Brown and Isaacs (2003) researched powerful questions with fellow practitioners. They sought to understand the architecture of powerful questions and discovered that they consist of three distinct dimensions:

- The linguistic construction of a question.

What is the first word of a question? Questions that start with why or how are generally more powerful than questions that start with what, when or where?

- The scope of the question.

How can we most effectively deal with stress in our team? or How can we deal with societal stress more effectively in the times we live in?

- The assumptions that are contained in the question.

A question becomes more powerful if it challenges existing assumptions. For instance: "How can we compete most effectively with the Chinese?" is less powerful than: "How can we best collaborate with the Chinese?" The second version is more generative as it invites a different way of thinking.

You can play around with these three dimensions while crafting or fine-tuning a question.

ASKING QUESTIONS IN THE MOMENT

Of course, not every question can be reflected on that long before you raise it. There are also situations in which you have to come up with a question instantaneously because you think that a particular question might help shift the conversation, or deepen it, or just because you are curious and interested and want to know more.

This on-the-spot crafting of questions is almost a different type of crafts-manship; sensing what is needed in a particular moment and formulating a question in a powerful way. Being aware of the different possibilities and the effects of specific questions might help you to be faster in the moment. Most of us are aware of the difference between open and closed questions. But it might help to also think of:

- Curious questions, for example: I am really curious about your approach; can you please tell me more?

- Appreciative Questions, for example: How did you manage to achieve that result?

- Confronting questions, for example: I have read your organizational mission statement, yet I haven't met many people today who seem to be familiar with it, do you recognize that?

- Action oriented questions, for example: What is the first thing you are going to do now?

Some questions touch the head, whereas others are more about feelings or intuition. It can be very powerful to play around with these differences.

ON GOOD CONVERSATIONS

In Appreciative Inquiry, the quality of the conversations that people have with each other is essential to bring about change or transformation. But what does a good conversation look like in an organization and what is needed to make it happen? We briefly want to explore conversations from a communication perspective in this chapter, without diving too deeply into communication techniques. Because we found that, if you know what really matters to you in a conversation, you can use that notion to shape or change your conversations (and avoid the standard patterns of work meetings, for example).

We want to stress that we write about conversations in the sense of actual moments in which people sit together. But even though we talk only about such face-to-face encounters, the basic principles that we discuss here can be applied to asynchronous conversations and other forms of communications as well (e.g. social media, e-mail messages, newsletters, magazines, internal websites…).

CORPORATE COMMUNICATION AND GOOD CONVERSATION; WHAT IS THE DIFFERENCE?

A few years ago, organizational scientist Boris Groysberg and communication consultant Michael Slind researched the changing nature of corporate communication. Their impression was that this work domain is changing radically because of economic developments, new ideas on management and global trends such as social media and globalization. After interviewing dozens of people with a communication background, they increasingly had the feeling that they were talking to the wrong people. What was changing in internal communication went much further than the area of corporate communication. They phrased it as: "The field known as communication, which had long been a discrete institutional function, was evolving at many companies into a constellation of practices that extends across the entirety of organizational life." (Groysberg & Slind, 2012).

They decided to cast a wider net and included line managers in their inquiry. They asked them about the way in which they communicated with their staff and colleagues and what their reasons were for using that style of communication. It appeared that more and more managers were increasingly aiming for a good conversation with their people. "More and more leaders today, we found, place a high value on forms of discourse and styles of interaction that have far more in common with the model of two people talking than they do with standard-issue corporate communication." In other words: managers understand and practice reciprocal conversations during which people connect, explore topics together and exchange insights, and they value these over one-way presentations or meetings. In communications with larger groups they try to model the qualities of a personal one-to-one conversation and they design meetings to give space to person-to-person connections and deeper conversations.

Both researchers were surprised about the extent to which managers appeared to be preoccupied with this theme and how it was intertwined with the search for new ways of organizing and leading. Becoming an agile, learning and open organization, asks for a fundamentally different way of interacting. Leadership is a conversation, is the conclusion of Groysberg and Slind (2012). Their research helped them to identify four aspects of communication that can be influenced in order to enter into good conversations. That is to say: conversations that increase connectivity, in which new ideas emerge, that contribute to the development of what is important for the organization and that enable people to experience a sense of ownership. We call these *generative* conversations.

INTIMACY

The first aspect of a generative conversation is intimacy, good conversations draw people closer to one another. This proximity can be fostered by behaviors such as listening attentively, making personal contact, and building mutual trust. Talking about personal experiences, sharing meaningful stories, requesting feedback on your own performance or showing some of your own uncertainties and questions as a manager, all contribute to a more personal atmosphere in conversations. Proximity in the physical sense is not always possible when people work at different locations or see each other infrequently. But even in those cases, this atmosphere can be present in a mental or emotional sense – indeed, it may be even more important, as making personal contact distinguishes a true conversation from the more formal business communication. Groysberg and Slind (2012) explain that this form of conversation shifts the focus from a top-down distribution of information (telling) to a mutual (sharing) exchange of ideas. It's less corporate in tone and more casual and it's less about issuing and taking orders than about asking and answering questions. It is less role-to-role and more person-to-person.

INTERACTIVITY

Perhaps the most essential feature of a generative conversation is its interactive character. A personal conversation is always an exchange of ideas, questions and opinions between individuals. If there is not a two-way flow there is not a real conversation, but rather a presentation, speech or explanation. The extent to which you succeed in talking *with* each other, rather than to or about each other is therefore very important. Interactivity makes a conversation open and fluid instead of closed and directional. There is a balance between asking and telling – by both parties. This interactive nature explains other key features of generative conversations, namely: unpredictability, messiness, creative possibility in combination with open-endedness and differences in viewpoints. True generative conversations are seldom finished in one occasion – they may be stopped and then restarted at a future moment or occur simultaneously in different moments and places.

INCLUSION

Working with emotional intimacy and interactivity opens the door for a third feature of powerful conversations: inclusion or togetherness. A conversation has more impact when influential ideas emerge from all sides, from managers and from staff, from inside and outside. Groysberg and Slind found that in genuine conversations that truly contribute to business performance and innovation, staff members provide substantive input to the discussions. Not only do they respond to the ideas from managers, they also contribute their own ideas, share their personal interests and see themselves as co-authors of an ever changing narrative – about what is going on and about next steps – and consequently become *thought leaders*, storytellers, and proud ambassadors of their organization or brand. In these conversations a different dynamic emerges than in settings where the vision is explained and assignments are handed over. The most important finding is that people generally leave a generative conversation ready to take action on ideas that they feel they have co-developed.

INTENTIONALITY

A final feature of generative conversations is that they have a clear focus. Groysberg and Slind call this: open but not aimless. People come together because of an aspiration, they want to organize, build, research, or learn something with others. There is a certain amount of purposefulness that provides energy and that explains why the conversation makes sense, is important to everyone and also provides a certain structure. You do not talk for the sake of talking, but because you want to *do* something together (Groysberg & Slind, 2012). In our experience, it is important that all participants share a feeling that there is something at stake, that they have something meaningful to take away or to do with each other. That is why the invitation to a conversation is so important. It can be very effective to ask everyone in the run-up to or at the start of the conversation: Why are you participating? What makes it important for you to show up here today? What do you hope will come out of the meeting?

All in all, we find these four aspects of generative conversation – intimacy, interactivity, inclusion and intentionality – helpful in designing, facilitating and influencing conversations in organizations.

LOOKING FOR A GENERATIVE DIALOGUE

A generative conversation does not happen automatically, nor is that always necessary or desirable in every context. Just like in our personal lives, we do not enter into a deep and profound exchange with everyone we meet. Otto Scharmer (2009) offers a useful model of four conversational patterns or phases that might all happen in a single conversation. The phases or patterns differ with regard to the amount of reflexivity, and to the outcome the participants seek – reasoning from the interest of the group and the whole – or more individually focused on their personal viewpoints and interests. Broadly speaking, the continuum runs from a polite exchange to creative flow – the most generative type of conversation. All types of conversations have their own contribution and role. Some conversations get stuck in a specific phase, while other conversations alternate between the different phases.

The model is a useful starting point for deciding how to facilitate a conversation, because it may help to pinpoint the type of interaction you are looking for. It also provides insight in what different conversation patterns require of participants. Furthermore, it indicates what you can do, as a facilitator, to keep the conversation going or to take it to the next level. In this chapter, we discuss this model as a tool for the facilitation and analysis of conversations.

FROM POLITE EXCHANGE TO CREATIVE FLOW

The conversational model of Scharmer distinguishes four fields that are presented schematically.

Polite Exchange

The starting phase is that of a polite exchange. Participants keep to the existing social conventions and do not yet freely speak their mind on what their thinking is or what is at stake. People discuss the agenda items, check who is present or not, and articulate what is already familiar. The established patterns and ways of interacting together all remain as they typically occur.

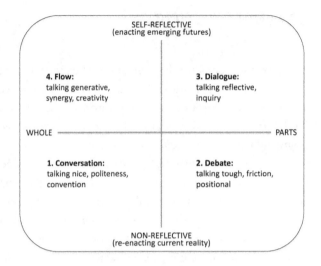

Conversation Model of Otto Scharmer
Source: Jos Kessels et al, 2002 (translated by authors)

During this phase you can positively influence the quality of the conversation, while at the same time respecting the polite exchange that is needed to establish a relational setting for an increasingly deepening conversation. One way to do this is to start sharing personal anecdotes, worries and personal interests as early in the conversation as possible. Our experience is that this approach prevents you from entering into what people know as typical meeting-mode. If you want to increase the interaction and intimacy, you should do this right at the start of the conversation. For instance, you can invite participants to exchange an inspirational moment of the past week with their neighbor. Or you can use the check-in to invite everyone present to respond to a question like: Why did you say yes to the invitation and decide to attend this meeting? Or What makes this meeting theme important for you? The sooner you begin this personal interaction, the easier the conversation will be later on.

Discussion

The second field of conversation – Scharmer calls this discussion or debate – is different from the first because participants start to express themselves by saying what they think. People share their opinions or ideas and discuss them with others. They exchange multiple and alternative viewpoints that question or challenge the existing way of doing things. As new questions are raised, interests and dreams of different parties come to the surface. This phase requires that participants dare to take a position, to state what they think, even if they discover they are the only one who sees the situation in that way (Kessels et al, 2002).

Discussions create a space for people to contribute their own perspective and ensure that several viewpoints and voices can be heard. This creates the divergence and confusion that is needed to make a step forward later on by recognizing that different opinions and viewpoints exist. This phase also helps to challenge existing practices and stretch people's thinking.

The conversation, however, can become unclear, even confusing, in this phase because there are so many opinions and voices. How can these ever be (re)connected? It is important to remember that in this phase, it is not only about the content, but also about process. By allowing different voices to be heard, the seeds for holding joint conversations are planted. People may sit at the same table, but they only *truly* enter the conversation by expressing what is important for them, by sharing their story or contributing their idea. And hearing multiple perspectives creates a broader frame of thinking. With Appreciative Inquiry you intentionally invite many stakeholders, in order to explore the question or issue from different perspectives and mobilize and involve everyone. You make use of this diversity by giving space to all the voices, without necessarily trying to develop consensus or find common ground. The point is that everyone voices their opinion or feeling, so that a rich collection of ideas and viewpoints emerges.

The art is to stay in an open exchange, with a collection of viewpoints and not to end up in a real debate. Jos Kessels states that a discussion or debate can be an excellent manner of collecting and appraising the different sides to an issue. However, we may lose our openness when we find ourselves in a conversation that is characterized by friction and opposition. We may begin to attack others' ideas to defend our viewpoint. It helps to leave space for all the different viewpoints and ideas by summarizing them or by articulating the differences and showing that these are allowed to exist.

Dialogue

Over time, a discussion can evolve into a dialogue. By that we mean an inquiring conversation, in which images are set next to, or opposite, each other and we begin to inquire into our own and the other participants' assumptions and principles. A dialogue is more reflective in nature than a discussion. This requires individual members and the group as a whole to make a shift from presenting their ideas to exploring others' points of view and listening with empathy by putting themselves in the others' positions (Boers et al, 2002). When the group does not do this naturally, you can invite them to do so: We now have sufficient ideas on the table, shall we examine them? You might even propose a specific structured method for this, such as an exhibition of ideas perhaps by posting the ideas on the wall, as works of art, with participants walking around and asking questions. Typically, people ask a lot of questions in this phase. Different thoughts start to get connected and people start seeing linkages, making more sense of the whole, and better understanding what is important to one another. This opens the door to the next conversational level.

Flow

The final state is called *flow*, or *generative dialogue*. This type of conversation is different from a dialogue in the sense that people make the step from examining each other's viewpoints to co-creation of new perspectives (Scharmer, 2009). Generative dialogue is all about new thinking and discovery. Fresh ideas develop, as well as overarching concepts that help the conversation move forward. Afterwards, people who were part of such a conversation often can't recall who developed a specific line of thinking. The idea was just there, it suddenly emerged, sometimes in the form of a metaphor or a concept; for an image expresses more than we can capture in words.

This type of conversation does not happen on a daily basis, these are the moments at which everything seems to come together, things seem to flow naturally, and new ideas emerge that invite you into action. Think of that one spontaneous brainstorm with colleagues or that off-site during which all pieces of the puzzle of the past year seemed to come together. This makes it a type of conversation that creates sustainable and generative connections between those present, both at an individual and group level. In hindsight, the people who were part of the conversation are usually able to recall those moments as significant, both because of the ideas that emerged and because of their impact on individual relationships and the group's cooperation.

ENCOURAGING A GOOD CONVERSATION

All four types of interactions described above are worthwhile and relevant for different purposes and contexts. In the more reflective and inquiring stages of Appreciative Inquiry, a discussion or a dialogue would fit well, whereas in the more active inquiring phases it would be helpful to create the type of conversation that Scharmer calls a generative dialogue or flow conversation. However, this cannot be forced or planned. You can try to encourage this, for example, by actively exploring each other's ideas during a discussion instead of reacting to them, and in this way taking the conversation to the next phase, but there is no magic switch.

It can be necessary to really intervene when a team is stuck in the repetition of established ineffective patterns. For example, if the same voices are always heard throughout the meeting, while others are not, or if the dissonant voice or alternative perspectives are quickly discouraged, or if blame is pinned on others or the system. It becomes even more complex if people are removed from their own feelings about a situation, if serious rumors are circling around, or if people feel threatened or unsafe. These are times when additional interventions are often needed before you are able to enter into a substantive conversation with each other. In other cases, the intentional design of the conversation and the use of collaborative methods, such as requesting people to interview each other, or setting up a short exhibition of ideas, can help avoid pitfalls in the conversation later on.

TO A DIFFERENT WAY OF COMMUNICATING

In the last section, we talked about a conversation as a phenomenon in itself and we listed a number of principles and practices that you can use to influence the quality of a conversation. Our experience is that if you practice having these types of interactions or conversations with a team or department, people will bring this way of being in conversation to other settings, for instance in the day-to-day conversations in the workplace that occur between meetings. Behaviors like asking questions, trying to place yourself in the other's shoes, inquiring and asking about personal experiences appear to transfer easily to other encounters. They then become an attitude and a way of communicating. Teams that have experienced an Appreciative Interview several times or that have experimented with brainstorming in an inquiring way, tend to treat each other differently afterwards. This is not just a mere side-effect, but a valuable outcome of intentionally experimenting with different conversations. Barbara Fredrickson and Marcial Losada (2005) identified a remarkable difference between the ways in which high-performing and low-performing teams communicate with each other. In their research, they compared the sales results with the internal communication of the team along three axes:

- Positivity: encouraging, appreciation, yes-and versus negativity: criticism, disagreement, yes-but

- Inquiring: asking questions like, I want to know exactly what you mean, versus stating their judgements or counter-arguments like, I want to tell you how it works.

- Internally focused: my agenda, my team, versus externally focused: external stakeholders, the context.

In high-performing teams, communication appeared to be predominantly positive and to have a balance between inquiring and stating, internal and external focus. Remarkably, the lowest performing teams were twenty times more likely to make statements than to enquire, and even thirty times more likely to focus on internal matters than on external matters. By paying attention to negative events and entering into discussions with each other about them, a team can get stuck in a negative way of seeing each other and talking depreciatively. The research does not claim a causal relation between the quality of interaction and the performance of teams, but there does appear to be a clear correlation between the two.

STORIES AS A CATALYST FOR CHANGE

The shortest distance between two people is a story, is a favorite statement amongst storytellers. Stories connect. Every community – village, team, family, organization, professional group – has their own, often retold, experiences. People exchange anecdotes and events at the coffee machine, in the school yard or beside the camp fire. Stories contribute to cohesion and play a role in learning, from and with, each other. Unknowingly, we share insights and knowledge in a way that is natural and situational. We also create new meaning and shared images of what is happening. Stories can contribute to energy and raise hope or increase the belief that change is possible. In Appreciative Inquiry we frequently invite people in all sorts of settings to exchange stories. It is a method for understanding how a system works that creates a foundation from which shared images of future possibilities can be developed.

WHAT IS A GOOD STORY?

Sharing stories comes naturally to humans. We start doing so from the moment we learn to talk. However, in organizations we often don't make use of this capacity. We tend to use abstract and general language. A marketing report on target groups and retail markets always contains a bulk of figures and general information, but quite often not a single picture of an actual client. A report on an employee job satisfaction survey presents averages and tables, shrouding the stories of staff members behind those figures. They are there, but they are not made visible.

The moment you invite people to exchange stories about things they have experienced or something that touched them, a different conversation develops. At the kick-off meeting for a new organization, the freshly appointed managers were asked to share, amongst each other, what they thought was important in leadership. At the beginning the conversation was quite abstract. They stacked important things on top of each other such as: have vision, pay attention to people, and celebrate successes.

About ten minutes in the meeting, one of the participants asked a colleague, Can you give me an example of how you do that? In response, this colleague shared a personal anecdote about a successful project, how proud he was and how he had organized a small party afterwards and the effect this had on his team. Immediately, the atmosphere of the conversation shifted; the levels of engagement and energy increased noticeably and the interaction became richer. One manager commented, "For me, celebrating successes is more than organizing a party or going out for drinks. I think it is important to do something substantive as well! For example, we wrote an article after we won an award. And I also believe it is important to acknowledge those small day-to-day successes. Just yesterday, I gave a compliment to…."

In this exchange of stories and perspectives, similarities in how these managers preferred to lead became clearer, as did the differences. Every story or opinion led to a small inquiry, "Oh, is that how it works for you?" or, "Hmm, what do I really think of that?" This is precisely the mechanism that is applied in Appreciative Inquiry.

So, when we talk about stories in this setting, we do not mean fictional or metaphorical stories, we refer to the sharing of actual events and bringing experiences and specific moments into the circle of the conversation. It is also not about the *corporate story* in the sense of an official common story. We are interested in all the different real-life, personal stories of the people that work in the organization.

Key features of a good story are:

- It stands on its own feet: there is a beginning, middle and an end.
- It is authentic (truthful).
- There is lead character who experiences something, plot twists and turns, and other narrative elements.
- It is personal.
- It evokes emotions or is told with emotions.

(Tesselaar & Scheringa, 2009)

CONNECTING STORIES

Encouraging people to tell one another stories helps to:

- use and connect all the available local knowledge and enable the whole group to better understand how the system operates and what is possible in the system

- engage and connect staff members, with each other and with the question, both at a rational and emotional level

In other words, stories have a connective and integrating effect as they allow information from different places and sources to come together and they leave space for both reason and emotion. Exchanging stories can lead to a strong understanding of both the overview and the details and increase community spirit. As an education consultant, Bas van den Berg and his colleagues state: "In a well-functioning community *shared understanding* and *shared values* are optimally present. Through telling stories both are nurtured. Empathy and an understanding of how the whole works can be understood and sensed by everyone, and that is essential." (Van den Berg et al, 2011).

To realize a change, it is often necessary for shifts to occur at different places in the system. From our position in the organization, we cannot always understand how things work elsewhere and how different parts of the system are interrelated. By exchanging stories with a large group of people from different parts of the organization, people can reach a better understanding of the interrelatedness and the whole. Even if nobody can produce a comprehensive description and explanation of the whole, at the end, everyone has a better intuitive understanding and a broader scope.

But the exchange of stories is more than the sharing of knowledge or information, it also impacts relationships. By listening to others' stories and being encouraged to share experiences, people's perception of one another changes; their confidence grows and their sense of belonging increases. Even if people differ in opinion, the interpersonal contact improves and that is important. After all, if you want to make a step towards transformation as a group, the mutual contact or connection is as important as knowing where you are headed. So, this connecting power of stories is very important, especially in the long run.

AN EXAMPLE: A BREAKTHROUGH IN A TOUGH ISSUE

A newly set up dual work/educational program faced a lot of difficulties. For example, students found it hard to combine work and learning. School provided them with practical assignments to complete during their internship, but they were already very busy in the workplace with job-related tasks. As a result, students struggled to find time to work on their school projects, which negatively impacted their academic success. In addition, the program did not appear to be properly adjusted to actual practice. Few graduates were hired into the positions for which they were trained which frustrated them and raised concerns at the national policy level. This educational program was developed to boost a new type of job role that was felt to be needed – if these new roles were not opening up, the program would not meet its purpose.

This was a complex question, involving many different stakeholders. Course managers, internship mentors, managers, policy makers and employers all tried to think of solutions within their own sphere of influence. Evaluation studies were done, conferences were organized, but nothing much changed. An afternoon of storytelling turned out to be a significant catalyst to the process. We came up with the idea of sharing stories after a meeting with the different parties in which we discovered just how differently everybody experienced the problem. It reminded us a bit about the story of the five blind men and the elephant, everyone sees but part of the whole. How could we create a setting in which everyone's scope was broadened, and invite people to work on solutions together, instead of focusing on their position?

The original participants invited a number of people from their networks for a half-day meeting, making sure that all parties would be present. During the afternoon three people shared their personal stories with the group. There was no analysis of patterns, no numbers, no trends, or averages, simply straightforward personal stories, vivid and heartfelt.

Participants listened to the story of a student who struggled during his internship, a recent graduate who was frustrated that he couldn't find a job, and a manager who had students and recent graduates in the new job roles in his team but was still struggling with the content of these new roles. Each spoke honestly of what they wanted most, but also what they struggled with, what they had achieved and where they did not succeed and what all of this meant to them personally.

Afterwards, the whole group entered into round table conversations. Although the information was not new – everyone knew that these problems existed, that was exactly why the meeting was organized in the first place – people spoke about it differently. They saw connections between the different problems and began to understand why, for example, smart solutions that they had thought of in school did not work out in practice. A simple adjustment in the curriculum would never, on its own, improve things in the work practice for their students. Moreover, the meeting participants were energized, especially by the tangible frustration of the student and the graduate, to look for solutions together. In the final round, during which people shared discoveries and came up with ideas for action, all sorts of collaborations across organizational boundaries emerged. Given the large size of the group, this surge in energy and determination was an impressive experience for everyone present.

The crux when exchanging stories in a larger group is inviting people from different parts of the organization to tell their personal stories and to have others reflect on those stories so each person can see and hear the different perspectives and connect this to their own anecdotes and experiences. Shared meaning gradually develops through this analogic dialogue, listening and searching for the connections or links between things. This can lead to energy for change, as people emotionally connect with the question and the solutions. The stories can be about positive or about negative experiences. If the overall memory of the story is positive or valuable, then the story itself can have ups and downs, trials, hurdles and peaks. What is important is that the stories are about the personal experiences related to a question or topic and that the stories reflect what the narrators feel is important and truly wish for.

SHARING STORIES

People can be invited to share stories in all sorts of ways. For instance, by inviting a small group of people to tell a story to a larger group, or with a World-Café approach, during which everybody exchanges stories at tables (Brown, 2005) or through interviews in pairs.

The entire process of exchanging stories does not necessarily have to take place in one single session. A health care organization, for instance, experimented with management stories at the fireplace. In this relaxed setting, small groups of managers regularly exchanged stories about the reorganization and their new role. They shared what they ran up against and where and how they managed to realize their new role.

At the WAIC 2012 (World Appreciative Inquiry Conference), experienced AI facilitator and researcher Gervase Bushe shared that he increasingly moves the telling of stories to the period *before* an AI gathering. Bushe has found that we benefit more from the stories, when people start telling them beforehand. We record these crisp and powerful stories and use them during the session as a spring board for our inquiry around the affirmative topic. At the start of the gathering, Bushe invites people to read the stories out loud, one by one, in small groups. After every story is read, there is a quick brainstorm to determine what associations and thoughts the story generated. Bushe emphasizes this is about sharing and not about analyzing. It is about using the stories as a spark for new ideas. He says, "Let the group read and brainstorm. My experience is that this method very quickly leads to results and one gains a lot of time."

Whichever design choices you make; the following points of attention are relevant:

- Paying attention to the *form* of the stories, it is important. In organizations, we are so used to talking in abstractions, statements and generalities that we quickly fall back into this mode. By offering a framework for their story or by interviewing people, you encourage them to really tell a story. The art is to apply some structure, in the sense of a backbone. For example, by providing some core questions: What happened, who was there, what was the effect, what touched you the most, when did it become exciting? The art is to provide a loose structure because the creativity and the person's own way of telling the story are what makes it come alive.

- Providing a sample story can be an effective way of setting the right tone. For example, share a hand out with different interviews from the field. Such initial stories can inspire and invite others to add their story and they implicitly offer a structure, which creates an easy way in for other participants to get into story mode.

- Questions that encourage listening and reflection are also helpful... Consider questions that move the thinking in the desired direction and strengthen engagement. "What touches you most in this story and why?" will have a different impact than: "What are the five most important arguments you have heard?" Well-chosen questions assist the group to enter into a creative and meaningful reflective process.

PROTOTYPING: CREATING SOMETHING TOGETHER

The Taos Institute is an international network and research platform for social constructionism. With principles such as *words create worlds* and *the action is in the interaction*, social constructionism provides important theoretical foundations for Appreciative Inquiry. At the 20th anniversary celebration of the Taos institute, a couple of years ago, its founders were asked about their thoughts on what the focus of social constructionism should be for the coming years.

David Cooperrider gave a speech with the provocative title: *Stop Dialogue, Start Designing*. This was a daring proposition in this worldwide group of researchers and practitioners of dialogue-focused approaches to change. In his speech, Cooperrider stressed that it is important to not stick to conversations only. AI is aimed at radical transformation, rather than incremental change. For that to happen, something needs to be *done*. Next to reflective inquiry we need research-in-action and experimentation. Especially in the Design and Destiny phases of AI, when the focus is on co-creating new approaches to further a transformation, concepts and methods from the world of (industrial) design can be used.

INQUIRING BY DESIGNING

In 2004, Bruce Mau, a Canadian designer, created an exhibition with the title *Massive Change*. One of the quotes from the corresponding book reads: "Massive change is not about the world of design; it's about the design of the world." In other words: design works on fundamental change and transformation. In an AI process the design phase is aimed at co-designing the organization of the future. The task is to make choices together to turn dreams into a reality. There are two central questions that support this process:

- Imagine that our dreams are turned into daily reality, what would that look like?

- Which aspects of our organization should we address to move towards the direction of our desired future?

These questions are intended to brainstorm on the organizational aspects that should be addressed and to identify possible leverage points; to identify which feasible change ideas will take us in the direction of the envisioned future that excites and unites us. After mapping possible actions and initiatives, the people involved choose topics for a subsequent design step. It can be helpful to identify selection criteria or to provide focus questions, such as:

- Which components will combine the smallest change effort with the biggest impact?

- Which elements can we easily do something about ourselves?

- Which elements generate the most energy and attention of the stakeholders?

- Which aspect or element brings the dream closest?

An example from our practice: In a community development organization, a brainstorm on possible initiatives to create a movement in the organization towards the direction of the desired future led to a mind map with 35 different proposals. Following this exercise, a selection was made based on the question: Which themes do we jointly select to take forward? The organization thought it important that everyone's voice be heard and acknowledged in this decision. Therefore, the choice was not made by the board of directors, but by all the colleagues who were present.

To create an overview of everyone's preferences, each participant received three stickers that they could use to indicate which ideas or proposals they felt were important. Every participant could decide how to use his/her three votes. The votes could be allocated over three separate ideas, or all votes could be given to the one idea that they thought was *really* important. After the voting, it became clear that there were seven ideas the whole group thought of as most powerful or promising. The first step towards selection had been made.

Next, the seven ideas were written on flip-charts and participants were invited to stand close to the theme that they personally would like to work on. The single criterion was group size. For a design team, at least four people were needed, and no more than twelve. When groups would get too big, people were asked to split up in two design groups.

To ensure that everyone could work on a design question or idea that they were truly interested in, we also provided a blank flipchart. Every participant had the opportunity to nominate a theme that they felt was missing. In this case, the sheet remained blank, but on other occasions, new ideas have popped up and if enough people step up to work on them, they are pursued.

A DESIGN STUDIO

After the selection process, participants form design groups and start working as architects, designers, and product-developers in order to make a prototype for their group's topic. You may organize a design studio for this. "What does it look like?" is the leading question to help the group focus on creating a physical and tangible design. A design studio consists of five phases, each with their specific energy and focus.

- *Personal connection with the design theme.* At the start, everybody is asked to briefly share why they chose this specific theme. "What appeals to you in this idea?" is the question posed. That information alone provides direction and focus for the design.

- *Inspiration and ideation.* The purpose of the first phase is to generate as many ideas as possible concerning the design question. Firstly, the group transforms the design theme into a design question framed as, "Just imagine that everything is possible, how might we then design a [design theme] with which we achieve [desired result]?" This question provided focus. Subsequently, the group is invited to think of as many ideas as possible. At first, the focus is on quantity. After the brainstorm, the group is asked to cluster and prioritize the ideas.

- *Rapid prototyping.* Prototyping means creating a tangible image of a concrete idea or cluster of ideas that was identified during the brainstorm. It is about making a concept or intention come alive. It is important to invite the participants to really *make* something, for example; a storyboard, a role-play, body storming, or a 3D-performance. You can pretty much create a prototype of anything: products, services, processes, spaces, client experiences, partnerships, et cetera. The challenge to the group is to design quickly and not get caught up in the frills and details. For this phase, it helps to have lots of different materials available to work with. Design groups don't have to limit themselves to one prototype.

- *Formulate an aspirational statement.* Once the prototype is finished, the group is asked to articulate the ambition of the prototype as concisely as possible. What will be achieved once this idea has been implemented? Their answer uses energizing words and concrete images of the results. We also find that these aspirations become more powerful/useful if they are worded in the present tense, as if we are standing in the future, describing what success looks like.

- *Action planning.* Lastly, the group develops a plan for the next steps. Who or what do we need to make this prototype come alive? What could be the very first step?

AN EXAMPLE: CREATING A NEW APPROACH FOR INTERNSHIPS

The director of a teacher training college asked us to develop a new internship concept, together with a group of teachers. The teachers had already discussed this several times among themselves. This had led to a consensus about the idea that internships should have a closer fit with the vision of strengths-based education adopted by the college. At the same time, the group had the feeling that something was needed to take them from thinking to action. So the director invited people into a design studio. The design question was the same for everyone: If everything that we have visualized in our thoughts and imagination were possible, how could we design an internship in which the strengths of students are recognized, addressed and developed to the fullest extent possible?

Small design teams of teachers from the college and a number of their peers from the field started brainstorming, clustering and selecting the best ideas. Next, each group was given a form as a design format for their internship ideas. One group designed a gathering at which students would be informed about the new internship concept. Another group started working on the information brochure for the strengths-focused internship. A third group worked on a role-play that demonstrated the ins and outs of an internship evaluation between a student, college mentor and their internship mentor. A final group developed a newspaper section containing contributions from different viewpoints on the new internship-idea.

After every group was done, they presented their prototypes. Following this, the participants were invited to respond to two questions:

- Which element/component of this prototype appeals most to you?

- What idea or suggestion do you have for this group that would make the prototype even stronger?

Thanks to this setup, participants really started working with each other. They went beyond merely exchanging opinions to building a joint product. The vision that they had spoken about so often, suddenly became tangible and real. They found that *by creating* something together, their mutual relations improved.

These examples illustrate how designing and creating something as a group creates a totally different energy than talking about a topic. Designing and creating together facilitates movement. You stop thinking about a specific subject and start *realizing* it – translating it into practice. Innovation specialists, including Tim Brown (2009) call this approach Design Thinking.

INTERVIEW: EDWIN SCHELLING – SENIOR AEROSPACE BOSMAN AND THERMAL ENGINEERING
AI CANNOT BE LEARNED. AI IS LEARNING.

Edwin Schelling is the Dutch CEO of two international companies: Thermal Engineering and Senior Aerospace Bosman in Barendrecht. These factories produce components for aircrafts. He is educated as a physicist: to explain why things are as they are. When it comes to managing organizations, he has learned quite the opposite: to start from the inexplicable that is typical of humans, and from the unpredictability of change.

EVERYONE IS A SOURCE OF POSSIBILITIES

The metaphor that I like to use for a team or an organization is that of a soccer team. You position people in the team based on their strengths and create a context for them to perform as well as possible. I look at the entire company this way, instead of a looking at a function or a role; I look at what people have to offer. Everyone is a source of possibilities. Nowadays we do much more justice to the strengths of people in the way we work within our company. We design jobs in such a way that we maximize space for someone to do what they are good at. That is the biggest turnaround that we have made. It's nothing less than a paradigm shift, both for me and for others. We used to work on the basis of very different beliefs of how you should organize a company, what work actually means, and our beliefs about people.

CREATING CONDITIONS FOR SELF-MANAGEMENT

This focus on strengths fits in with a larger movement that we are making around self-management. When I joined Bosman as a director, there were many islands. People did not collaborate and there was a long tradition of top-down management. Partly because of this, we had major problems in our production. For example, our delivery times were far too long and I thought that we couldn't pick them up without changing the way we manage and organize things. That's why we started experimenting with self-management and with Appreciative Inquiry.

We observed that it worked, and I firmly believe that this approach to management and work is much more future proof. Look at the characteristics of today's young people. From them, you can deduce the characteristics of our organizations of tomorrow. The youngsters I see know what they are capable of and they are more self-assured. They believe more in developing their talents, in doing jobs that they believe in and their thinking starts from possibilities and opportunities. The management of our organizations needs to change because of this; we need to focus on enabling people to deploy their strengths and assist them in making smart decisions.

It is for that reason that I want to focus on creating a more horizontal organization with fewer fixed structures. We do not need more structures and protocols; we need clarity on the expected results and criteria with which people can organize their work. I envision more fluid careers in the years ahead, in which people take on a role for a specific period of time. Teams are important as they provide a context for collaboration. Becoming a team organization instead of maintaining a classic organizational structure is not an easy process. We need to overcome various barriers and transform our way of thinking. Instead of adapting the people to the existing system, we reversed the logic. We asked ourselves: If these are our people, what is the system that they need in order to perform well and for us to become a champion organization?

SUSTAINABLE CHANGE IS UNSTOPPABLE ENERGY

In this entire process of focusing on strengths, self-management and teamwork, I have gained a wealth of knowledge about my leadership and my implicit beliefs. Throughout my professional career, I have mainly worked in change management. The first thing I have always done is create buy-in and backing for an idea to the extent that a sufficiently large group would say: Let's try this! The AI-perspective on change has shown me a different starting point. Rather than convincing people, I now address their strengths, and I invite them to co-create the future from that strength. When I succeed in mobilizing people so that they start taking initiative and responsibility to the extent that it cannot be stopped; that is when we have achieved sustainable change and that is what I truly need in the long run. In the past, after completing a successful change project

I frequently doubted how long the change would last. Backing and support are not enough to create transformation. Transformation requires true engagement and personal initiative.

AI AS A JOURNEY OF DISCOVERY

My current dream is to change Thermal Engineering in such a way that I can say: The AI approach is our way of dealing with things. If we can manage this, I would love for others to come and visit us, so that I could explain to them how we managed to achieve this by trial and error. If there is one core lesson that I have learned, it is this; AI cannot be learned, AI is the learning! It is a discovery tour. I have failed to find a useful blueprint anywhere. This was incredibly stretching for me. Attempting something in a conventional manner and failing is much easier explained and accounted for. Doing something in an unconventional manner feels quite different. During this process, some people told me: Edwin, forget it. It's never going to work. It really felt like swimming against the current, I realized that if I failed, I would have a lot of explaining to do...

FROM THE TRUTH TO JUST MY TRUTH

In this process I have pushed my boundaries. I have learned to let go, to exercise patience, to respond to bottom-up initiatives as opposed to adhering to my own ideas. My faith in the goodness and competence of people helped with this. Everyone can take a good decision once they are given the correct tools and information. I have always maintained that stance, and it has really been confirmed by my experiences.

Besides that, my own determination played a significant part. I really *wanted* our way of working to be different from the conventional ways. As a manager, I have been educated in a specific way of thinking. However, increasingly I experienced limitations to this approach. I simply *felt* that things were not as they should be. Questions crept up on me. Should I always take the lead? Is letting go so dangerous? What is it that I am accountable for? And what do we expect of employees? This entire experience made me re-examine my own assumptions on leadership. The change process has become a personal discovery tour of my trusted approaches and assumptions and freed me up to make choices anew.

TOOLKIT: APPROACHES AND METHODOLOGIES

APPRECIATIVE INTERVIEWS

The appreciative interview is possibly the most frequently used intervention in Appreciative Inquiry and one that can be applied in many different ways and situations. Diana Whitney and Amanda Trosten-Bloom pinpoint it as a keystone of every AI-process because it goes to the core. It sets up an inquiring conversation about energetic situations through sharing personal stories and using curiosity as a driving force to construct collaborative new knowledge…. In this chapter we explore how you can set up and use appreciative interviews. How does it work? How do you come up with a good design? When can you use appreciative interviews?

DISCOVER OR DEFINE

With an appreciative interview you invite people to have an inquiring conversation on an important positive (affirmative) topic. Typically, such conversations occur during the Discovery phase. For instance, if you want to start an inquiry in a school on high impact interactions in the classroom; conversations in which students learn much, feel engaged and energized, you could ask teachers and students to interview one another about moments that they experienced such interactions. With the help of a short interview format people can easily enter into conversations with each other, exchange stories and explore these stories further to learn about the topic. We provide an example format in the frame below. Of course, there are many possible variations.

APPRECIATIVE INTERVIEW - OUTLINE

Interview – in pairs

Think of a situation, an experience:

A moment that you remember, during which you intentionally or by accident [identify the positive topic in detail, e.g.: had a conversation in class between teachers and students in which you felt energized, engaged and learned new things]. An example of [affirmative topic, e.g. high impact conversations] that energized you.

Use the following questions for your inquiry:

- Please briefly describe the situation and tell me the story (who, what, where, etc.)

- What were you doing in that situation? (especially: What did you do that worked?)

- What was the effect of your contribution or participation? (on others, on yourself, on the work/growth/achievements?)

- How do you remember feeling at that time?

- What makes this moment so memorable for you?

- What does this story say about your and other's strengths related to [affirmative topic], and about other key success factors? What is important to keep in mind?

Appreciative interviews can also be applied one stage earlier in the process, in the Define phase, when you are still looking for the affirmative topic. While working with a team of Workers' Union representatives that was unhappy about their current teamwork and focus, we asked them: Can you recall the moment that you joined the Union? How and when did that happen? Do you remember what your dreams and aspirations were at that time? What did you want to achieve, or what contribution did you dream of making? We invited people to relive those moments and share those anecdotes: When did you decide to join? Where were you at that moment? Do you remember your first meeting? What was on your mind then? In sharing those stories and by interviewing each other about those memories, their original drive to work for the Union quickly came to the surface, which in itself influenced the spirit of the group ("in essence, we are in this with the same dreams and drive...!").

This sharing also gave a vantage point to focus the subsequent inquiry. The affirmative topic became: How can we regroup, refocus, in order to really make a positive difference for the workers we represent? Or, more briefly: How can we make a positive difference together? In the ensuing Discovery phase, we *again* made use of appreciative interviews. This time the key question was: Can you share a story about your time in the Union when you made a positive difference that mattered to you and energized you? By exploring these stories, the group got a better sense of what type of difference they could make and what that takes.

Appreciative interviews can be elaborate or very brief. They can function as a first step in an AI process or as an intervention in its own right, or even as a warm-up question.

AN EXAMPLE: APPRECIATIVE INTERVIEWS ON THE ISLAND OF CURACAO

An experience of setting up a more elaborate process with appreciative interviews is a project we worked on, that focused on the future of the island of Curacao (Kabalt, 2012). The basic vantage point was that there was a general feeling that the island's inhabitants weren't very proud of Curacao and that the population in general lacked self-confidence, a sense of clear identity, and faith in the future of their country. This was a problem since it contributed to a trend of young people tending to emigrate instead of investing in their future at home. We sought to inquire into whether it was possible to spark a different type of conversation on the future of the island.

Fifty youngsters from Curacao participated in the project. They attended a short training in appreciative interviewing, and then each of them interviewed five inhabitants of Curacao, ranging from the former prime minister to a grandfather. They asked questions like: What is your dearest memory of Curacao? What would you want Curacao to be like, twenty years from now? Afterwards, the young interviewers came together to share what they had heard and learned from the conversations. They were particularly surprised by all the beautiful stories and examples from the interviews. As one remarked: Normally you just hear negative stories, but it *is* possible to appreciate ourselves and other island people. Remarkably, their perspective of the island had already shifted through these conversations. They had become more proud of their island, and felt more connected because they had discovered that the population was far more united in their dreams and drive than they had thought. In addition, they were inspired to do something for Curacao themselves.

FOCUSING AN APPRECIATIVE INTERVIEW

When an appreciative interview is used as an integral part of a larger AI process, as in the example above, the affirmative topic is usually the focus of the interview. But it is also possible to use appreciative interviews as a more stand-alone intervention. For instance, at the start of a leadership development conference in your organization, you can pose the question: Tell me about moments in which you as a leader were totally in your element? Or, at the start of a project on partnership with external stakeholders to get more focus on what it is that people mean by partnership, you can ask: Tell me about a moment in which you experienced true partnership.

Whenever or however you use an appreciative interview, it is essential to have a clear focal point. When an appreciative interview becomes too general (Tell me about a success) this may lead to a positive conversation, but it will not be very effective as an intervention. More than that, it might even be detrimental to the process if people feel there is a problem in the collaboration, and they are invited to talk about successful teamwork or about things that do go well. They might feel the conversation is missing the point entirely and become irritated or disengage.

Focusing the appreciative interview on the theme that you want to take forward makes it powerful. Imagine, for example, that you want to apply AI to guide your team development process. An effective central question could then be: Tell me about an inspirational experience of collaboration in this team (or any team you have been in) followed by: When did you feel happiest, most proud, energized and supported by your team members?

But the following could also work: Tell me about the most challenging experience that you ever had in your team – when you felt highly stretched, the stakes were high, and you received constructive feedback and inspiration from your team members that helped you through the situation.

Or: Tell me about a moment in which you felt strongly connected to your team members, on a common purpose; you were clearly all working on the same theme, in a way that made you feel part of a larger whole.

As you can imagine, a series of other questions could work as well. It really depends on what you want to inquire about… Whether or not a particular question hits home depends on how much it touches upon the actual topic at hand. So it is important to choose your central question with care, and perhaps even try out a few different questions to see which one works best.

The *Encyclopedia of Positive Questions* (Whitney et al, 2014) lists a wide-ranging assortment of subjects on which you could conduct an appreciative interview – from client satisfaction to strategic planning. The book consists of a large collection of interview guides that have been used in projects all around the world. Even though the content differs, there are a number of similarities that are noteworthy across the examples:

- Every interview guide starts with an introduction of the theme. The theme is explained positively in a few sentences to provide context.
- The number of questions is limited – three to five, on average.
- The questions invite respondents to share experiences and inquiries.
- The questions aim to identify and explore (inquire in) actual situations and anecdotes. This is to avoid speaking in generalities (e.g. I just happen to like working with different people. I always think trust is a necessary prerequisite to good teamwork.) Powerful questions ensure that people share stories and anecdotes.

The power of an appreciative interview depends on the questions we pose, next to, of course, the attention and concentration with which the actual conversation then takes place.

THE ROLE OF THE INTERVIEWER/LISTENER

Recounting personal experiences and reflecting on them is easier when someone is listening attentively. Even if that someone is paper (a diary or notebook) or an animal (a pet dog or the stuffed animal you had as a child). The fact that someone is *listening* is essential to telling a story. Brenda Ueland (1998; p. 51) describes this very aptly: Listening is a magnetic and strange thing, a creative force... When we are listened to, it creates us, makes us unfold and expand. Our story comes to life by telling it to someone. By sharing their stories, storytellers give meaning to their own experiences and discover new elements that they were previously unaware of (see: Milton Erickson in Rosen, 2010; Reynolds, 2011). This happens, in part, because people respond to each other. A brief silence on the part of the listener/interviewer makes the person telling the story think through his or her own words a little bit better (what did I say, exactly?). A slight nod may encourage us to investigate a small part of our story further – to look for more discoveries, to delve even deeper. In a way, the story exists not only within, but also between people. Especially when the listener does not judge, evaluate, assume too much, fix, solve problems, give advice or applaud... but leaves the story with the one who tells it (Swart, 2016).

People are born storytellers, and also born story-listeners. Our brain is very well equipped to digest information in the form of anecdotes, stories and examples. Listening to stories usually triggers stories that are buried in our own memory, similar experiences. That is why people who hear a story tend to start sharing their own stories... Therefore, it helps to give people conducting appreciative interviews, clear instructions. For example:

- Take turns interviewing each other, 10 minutes per person
- Let's listen to each story for 5 minutes before responding or asking more questions.
- Try to visualize someone's story as you are listening to it and explore it from that point of view.
- Be as curious and open minded as you can be, pretend you are a 4-year old, wanting to know everything about this situation.

APPRECIATIVE INTERVIEWS ARE DIFFERENT

An appreciative interview is different from a normal interview conducted by, for instance, a Master student for his thesis, a journalist for an article or a consultant who wants to analyze a certain organizational issue.

Firstly, appreciative interviews are explicitly concerned with the moments in which something actually worked in a way that energized people – even if these moments were only a positive exception-to-the-rule. People are invited to share stories that, for them, are truly relevant.

Secondly, an appreciative interview is – as opposed to many other forms of interviewing – not exclusively aimed at the collection of information or input. It is just as much about establishing relations between the stakeholders and generating energy and self-confidence that will mobilize people. The process is at least as important as the content.

Interviewers in appreciative interviews are perhaps best described as listeners and co-inquirers. They try to find the gold (in the sense of qualities, capabilities, working principles) that lie in the experience being shared.

WHO INTERVIEWS WHOM?

The interviews are typically most powerful when conducted in a one-on-one situation during which the interviewer listens with genuine curiosity to the story of the other. This can be arranged for in a very large group by asking the participants to conduct conversations in pairs. Because the sharing of stories impacts the quality of the relations, the most powerful interviews generate new connections. Either by connecting people who normally don't share much information (such as a teacher interviewing a student on powerful learning situations) or inviting people who already work together to share a side of themselves that their colleague doesn't know (such as sharing the story of your first working day as a Workers' Union member).

This brings up the "who" question. If you want to get going with appreciative interviews, there are several (Whitney & Trosten-Bloom, 2010):

- Who conceives the interview questions?

- Who are we going to interview?

- Who will conduct the interview?

But also:

- How many interviews can each interviewer conduct?

- What type of training, explanation or instruction do the interviewers here need?

The question who interviews whom is very important. For an AI process to be rich it is crucial to involve the whole system in the process. Not literally in the room perhaps – but at least in the process. The underlying working principle is that something emerges between the people conducting the interview. When two people from one team have a conversation about the most powerful collaboration moment with an external partner, something different happens than when two people from *different* teams have that exchange or when a team member *and an external partner* reflect on powerful collaboration moments. All three possibilities can be worthwhile. The key point is to decide what you are after. In designing the process, it is important to consider the effects of different possible combinations of people.

WHAT TO DO AFTER THE INTERVIEWS?

Conducting the appreciative interviews is already an intervention it its own right and at the same time it is – especially if you are working with large groups – valuable to analyze and share the stories that appear in the interviews without taking the zest out of them. Important questions when working with large groups or even with entire organizations are:

- How do we analyze and share the findings (are we actually going to do that?) and who will assume this responsibility?

- How do we communicate the stories from the interviews to the other stakeholders?

Different approaches are possible in order to make sense of the many conversations and to see patterns in the stories. For example, reading the stories one by one in small groups, until no new themes emerge is a practice we learned from Gervase Bushe. Another way is to explicitly ask for those stories and quotes that have remained with the interviewers or that touched them the most, and to build on those to seek patterns. In any case it is a *qualitative* analysis in which the strength and richness of the individual stories is preserved.

Following this exercise, it is a challenge to find a way to share insights from the interviews with the organization, using a film, posters in the canteen, an event, a magazine... Whatever you do, ensure that group of people who shared the stories still recognize their stories as their own, including their language and their examples. Only then, will they be able to build on them. If the summary results in a well-analyzed report or polished corporate story, it will lose its power as a driver for the next steps.

LOOKING BACK TO TAKE A STEP FORWARD: THE POWER OF A HISTORY TIMELINE

Working with Appreciative Inquiry means hopping, skipping and jumping through time, in a somewhat irregular sequence: dreaming of the future, talking about the now, analyzing the past. A powerful manner of playing with the latter is making a history timeline. This can help a team or group to look at their process and the organization as an evolving story, in which they can write the next chapter. This brings energy for change to the fore and fosters both motivation toward and a perspective on, the future. How does this happen? Why does it work? We will start with an example and subsequently explain the method.

AN EXAMPLE: A TEAM IN A TIGHT SPOT

A powerful experience of working with a history timeline was with a team that was stuck in multiple ways. There was hesitation at the start of the session. Team members sat with their arms crossed and waited for the team day to start. Their body language demonstrated that they did not have high expectations nor were they motivated. The new team leader had already mentioned this and it was the principle reason for planning this day.

The relationships and collaboration within this group of fifteen case managers were poor and this affected everyone, but no one felt strong enough to counter the tide. Even the team leader was unsure of the way forward. For some time, the team had operated without a manager. As the new team manager, he was reluctant to just step in and start working. The group meeting was important for him to ensure a healthy start. We chose the history timeline as a way to connect.

First, we asked the group to stand on a straight timeline in a chronological order that showed when they joined the team. The man who had been working there the longest was first, the new team leader, who had just entered a few weeks ago, was at the end of the timeline. With some joking and jesting about ages of people, everyone found their place. They broke up in groups of four in which they considered the question: What important events have you been part of? What stories do we need to know if we want to understand the story of this team? If you were to write a book about this team, which moments should be in it? This led to lively discussions in the small groups. Each group then wrote their most significant moments on blank sheets of paper. In a plenum, these stories were shared by placing them on a room-wide brown paper, one by one. In conversation we constructed the team's history timeline. We shared stories, anecdotes, moments or periods of time – a true reconstruction of the whole process. At times we needed to look for a date or reconstruct the chronological order of events. ("No, that was after Joyce departed, I am sure, we had just received those new desks and she never worked on those!") Such sharing contributed to a different type of conversation.

Gradually, as the shared narrative unfolded, the pattern that had emerged in this team became apparent to all. Their story included hair-raising incidents of a manager who became ill and later passed away, a substitute manager who had a heart attack in the office, budgets that were frozen because nobody represented their team in the (annual) budget meetings, dangerous client situations (the team worked with homeless people, including many with addictive and psychiatric problems) and colleagues who dropped out.

There were also many positive memories: a new colleague who joined to strengthen the team, a summer during which the team was understaffed and everybody joined in to keep the ball rolling and people juggled resources and hours just to ensure the support for clients, and a client who managed to get back on his feet again and came to say goodbye in a heart-warming manner. Participants listened carefully to each other and assisted one another in the reconstruction: Yes, I remember that, and then you came over to help me as well! A colleague expressed her anger about the way she had been treated by an interim manager and was relieved that she could finally tell her side of the story without anybody opposing her or attempting to give her advice. All eyes were turned towards the room wide brown paper, as the focal point. This focus created a different conversation than the group had ever had. People did not talk to each other, but with each other, constructively.

Two hours later the history timeline was finished. We concluded with a summary of a few story lines and themes and the closing question: What do you feel should be the next chapter in the history of your team? You could hear a pin drop, when an older, relatively quiet, colleague spoke out: When I listen back to all that we have gone through and I see how it still affects us, then I think we have simply just had too much on our plate. Too much for any team whatsoever, and instead of us rallying to support each other, it managed to divide us. We have become uncertain, fearful and angry. In addition, to survive or to just keep standing, we started fighting for our own little island. By taking that route we managed to lose each other. Our next step should be that we start connecting again, supporting each other to face the external challenges in an effective manner. The team was quiet because this was spot-on. Their colleague had voiced the general sentiment of the group and in that moment, the group felt more connected than they had for a long time.

Impressed by the stories and the emerging sense of team we parted ways. The following week we would meet the team again, to plan for next steps. Three days later the team leader called us. Two of the team members would not be present at the follow-on day; they had requested a transfer and shared their reasons: "Clearly, this team wants to take the next step, but for us too much has happened. I am afraid that we cannot fully participate in the team, too much has happened here for us which means we would frustrate further development, something we don't want to do. We would rather start afresh in new positions." Making the history timeline had served to prepare them for a next step, as it did for the others; only for them it meant a step out of the team.

This example illustrates one of the many different ways in which a history timeline works and what its potential is. By collecting important experiences, the group (re)constructs its own collective story. That helps people who have been around for some time to start seeing patterns. Those who have only a short history with the team gain valuable insights and a sense of shared ownership. Furthermore, everyone gets an overview, precisely because of the web of stories, and arrives at a shared perspective. Instead of being in the movie, people watch the movie. That is why the conversation works like a stepping stone for new developments. People develop a deeper understanding of what is happening and gain more faith and confidence in the next step. To quote the French poet Aragon, *I have reinvented the past to be able to see the beauty of the future* (Aragon, 1963).

WHAT MAKES IT WORK?

One of the core principles behind AI is the poetic principle; an organization can be seen as a structure, but it can also be seen as a self-propelling story; an open book that everyone contributes to (Cooperrider et al, 2003). By adopting a perspective that incorporates a past and a future; ownership, connectivity and energy emerge. Van den Berg and colleagues who frequently use stories to work in schools describe this: The story that is told about a school goes deeper if the history and the future expectations resound in it. When parents, teachers and pupils have the feeling that they live in a building, a building that is alive, that has a history, they are eager to learn and work there (Van den Berg et al, 2011).

Through the process of sharing anecdotes, without drawing a conclusion or reaching a resolution, a conversation emerges within the team that we can capture as narrative space (Kessels, 2002). This is a form of dialogue in which everyone participates and looks for what is present and how the situation of the team could be understood in different ways. Participants enter into an inquiring, non-judgmental mindset: What is happening here? In what way do my colleagues experience the situation? What different views are held on this collaboration of ours? What's at stake for everyone? What patterns have we developed together?

In a very matter-of-fact way, that dialogue is appreciative; it values shared and individual experiences in the sense that everything is allowed to be there. Because the dialogue is a reconstruction of what happened, there is no need to fix things or resolve issues. Looking back at a situation or talking about an incident from the past, sharing how you and how others experienced it, investigating the part you yourself played in it, is easier in retrospect than when the situation is on-going.

Another important principle is that of continuity. In his book *Built to Last*, Jim Collins shows that successful organizations are very good at changing, *while* keeping the essence of the organization intact. Change is good, but first know what we should not change (Collins, 1994). Knowing what your core is, your DNA as an institution, is very important. A history timeline can serve to illuminate the core in a manner that facilitates shared sense making and understanding of the system.

Constructing a history timeline in a hospital we were working with, revealed that nuns had established the institute. Originally, it was more of a nursing home, and no matter how much had changed over time with the institute developing into a hospital, these roots of caring and nursing were still tangible. This realization gave a different perspective of the future and the intended merger with an academic hospital with firm roots in research and science. It made it possible for the hospital step into that collaboration process with a clear sense of identity.

THE HISTORY TIMELINE PROCESS

In developing a history timeline with a group there are many possible ways to go about it. The basic approach is:

- Determining focus and purpose is the first step. Is the focus on evaluating a specific period or is it a more general reflection in preparation for a subsequent phase?

- Participants position themselves in the order of their entry in the group – this is usually a dynamic moment because participants are often unaware of each other's start date. Sometimes it leads to an explicit and renewed recognition of everyone's position in the system.

- In groups of three or four, participants exchange anecdotes and decide which stories and incidents should be included when they write the history of their organization/ team/ project group. Their stories are written on a blank page.

- All anecdotes (pages) are placed in a chronological order on a timeline. While placing the stories they tell the whole group the story so that as more pages are put on the timeline the whole story begins to emerge.

- At the end, the group reflects on questions, such as: What can we learn from this? What threads can we see? What is the next step going to be? What is at stake?

The group can be large or small, you can work on the history timeline for two hours or the entire day. These choices depend on the context and the purpose (Bunker & Alban, 1997). You can also decide not to do this at one specific moment but turn it into an on-going inquiry that involves a large part of the organization. In that way an entire company's *learning history* can be crafted

(Smid et al, 2006). Of course, the other extreme is possible too. One person can make a history timeline for the organization. The Chair of the Board of a large college for vocational education decided to start a management conference on the multi-year strategy for his institution with the story of how the school had developed – including old slides and artefacts (such as writing pads and old letter heads). The current school had originally consisted of five different legal entities that were reluctant to be joined together, but for reasons of survival, they finally did take that route. At the beginning it was more a marriage of convenience (united we stand, divided we fall), but after eight years the Chair was keen to establish more connectivity and he wanted to adopt the management principle of working as one school. Because in his opening address, the Chair revisited the origins of the five very separate and autonomous institutions and shared stories that highlighted their different qualities, the managers were open to his approach. He also shared some stories of the past eight years that made the managers aware that they already had a history together. They were no longer five separate entities! Everyone felt seen and heard with their own shared story. *That* is also the power of the history timeline.

CAN YOU SEE IT? ENVISIONING THE DESIRED FUTURE

When engaging in a change process by building the bridge while walking on it, experimenting and discovering your path along the way, it is important to feel a strong pull from the other side. That is what provides the motivation and drive to get to work, to explore, broaden your horizon and try out new things. It also gives direction, like a North Star. Peter Senge calls this sensation creative tension: The gap between vision and current reality is also a source of energy. If there were no gap, there would be no need for any action to move towards the vision. We call this gap *creative tension* (Senge, 1990). If we can imagine the vision, we can change or move toward it.

In AI we work with envisioning and dreaming in order to evoke this tension. It is not about one person sharing his or her vision for the future, however inspiring that vision might be, but about creating a setting in which everyone envisions what it is like to be in that (best possible) future, however briefly. Dwelling on best experiences from the past creates the perfect springboard to dream freely and use your imagination. The art is to make it feel like you are already in that desired future.

ACT AS IF YOU ARE ALREADY THERE

The American conductor Benjamin Zander (2002) rewards all his students with an A at the start of his course. His only condition is: Write me a letter in the next two weeks, dated in May – at the end of this semester – in which you articulate why you have received that A. It is essential that the students write this letter as if it is already May. They do not write; I hope by then I have… or Maybe in May I will have learned that…. Instead, what they write is something like: It is now May and I have grown immensely over the past months. Consequently, they explain how they have grown, where they are now and what this means to them. All of this happens in their imagination.

Why does Zander (2002) do this? He explains: I have struggled for years with the stress of students at the start of the course. Even if I tried to calm them down by saying that everyone would pass the course – there were always students who doubted themselves. They held back because of this. By not saying: You will probably receive an A. You will graduate, but by effectively rewarding them the A already, the students react in a fundamentally different way. They are less preoccupied with how they are assessed and what Zander, as their teacher, thinks of their performance. Instead, they are focused on themselves and what they can be and what they can achieve which dares them to think bolder and bigger and greatly enhances their learning.

POSITIVE IMAGE, POSITIVE ACTION

For exactly the same reason, in AI we invite people to dream and imagine after they have reconnected with their shared strengths or best practices related to a topic they have chosen. At a lecture during WAIC 2012, Ron Fry shared: The function of the Dream-phase is, for me, the stretching of thoughts; you will see a bigger whole and new possibilities. It works well to use tangible and visible products to support this process. Most AI-facilitators therefore invite people to create something in this phase: a collage, a movie, a poster, a performance. The importance and power of these products is mostly that they are *made*. The materializing of our imagination is an important step towards transforming our intentions into action. It is therefore not so much about whether you think a collage is beautifully made or not, or if you are exactly going to realize a certain dream vision. It is about the experience that the creation of those images brings with it. We sometimes call this creating a memory of the future. A future image that is so powerful that you (a) feel an appetite to move towards that future and (b) believe that is possible to get there. You explicitly create a tangible tension between where you are now and where you want to be (and believe you can be). A positive image of the future helps you to develop into that direction, positive image, positive action is what David Cooperrider calls this fundamental AI principle (Cooperrider, 1999).

It is, in fact a form of experiential learning, but different because you are learning from an experience that is ahead of you (and that you will perhaps never actually experience in that exact way) rather than from an experience that is behind you. This is essential for issues for which we need to think of solutions before they actually occur. Hilary Bradbury (Verheijen & Dewulf, 2004) argues that there are some issues in our society for which we cannot afford to have a lot of hands-on (trial and error) experience; we need to do something about it *now* and learning from future experiences can accelerate that process.

In order for it to work, dreaming about what can be should build on a process step in which stakeholders have connected and reflected on strengths and successes. The dream session becomes a type of extrapolation: Imagine it was always like that, what would it look like? What would be the core of how you would work? You can shape this envisioning phase in different ways:

- A visualization using the miracle-question: Imagine you wake up after this weekend and somehow a miracle happened at work, everything is at its best. What do you see when you enter the building? What do people say to each other?

- Create a collage of images, individually or in a group.

- Work with images or photographs.

- Invite people to take photographs or create a movie.

- Write a letter.

- Tell a story.

- Enact a performance.

The possibilities are endless. A person we work with who trains actors sometimes invites people to fast-forward the movie and imagine it is a year later: If you are doing the work that you love to do, just like you explained to us in the interviews, what would I see you do? Act out the scene now.

Lots of different forms work, but it is important to make sure that the form fits with the group, that it evokes a response from them and that it draws upon the power of imagination. "We know more than we can tell", is how psychologist Polanyi described it. Metaphors and images help to express that for which we have no words (yet) and tap into our tacit knowledge (Polanyi, 1966).

Years ago, we supported a back-office team that found itself in a rough patch. There was a lot of pressure to improve their performance. We intentionally chose a number of playful forms to envision so that we could invite them to test the water with their toes, rather than inviting them to dive right in, because that would have been too much of a stretch for them. The team was too insecure about whether they had it in them to create the needed improvement. We made several snapshots of the future. One of the activities was writing testimonials from their internal and external clients: It is one year from now and we interview clients about our service delivery, what do they say? This was one of the moments that got the team going. In no time, the whole flip-chart sheet was filled with statements. A year later we found this exact sheet that had been rolled up and forgotten on the filing cabinet of the team leader and the surprise and emotion of the team was huge when they realized that it was no longer as far away as they initially thought it would be for clients to say things like this about them. Indeed, some of those statements had been made by clients already.

It does not always turn out that way, nor does it need to. Envisioning the future is not about creating an ideal image that you consequently implement step by step. It is important to create an image that increases your belief in a positive future and creates a productive tension between that and the current state, which in turn evokes the energy to get going and come up with first ideas for action. From those images you can establish a link with the present: Which actions or initiatives will help us to take steps in the direction of our desired image of the future starting today?

Shouldn't all those images be integrated into one common image? We are used to striving for one shared vision that unites everybody. Ron Fry is quite clear about this: "Strive for alignment rather than agreement among those concerned." is his advice. It is helpful if the different dreams do not contradict each other, and if they loosely fit together when it comes to the direction they are heading, but people can disagree on certain aspects or have a slightly different dream for the future. When you continue to keep the conversation about the future alive over time, you can continue to work with these different needs and wishes. The whole idea behind AI is, of course, that it is not a one-shot intervention, but an inquiring process that you create and shape together. It is therefore not just about creating a single shared dream together, but about inviting people to envision their own dreams and kick start their own energy for change. By articulating the affirmative topic or the opening question in such a way that it provides direction, the dreams will automatically be interrelated in one way or another. That is why we do not insist on unity at the start of the dream phase, but rather see how the different dreams sit together *at the end* of the dream phase. If there is a lot of difference between the different dreams, this is worth discussing: What does it mean that we have such different dreams and how much difference or commonality do we want, and why?

EXPERIMENTING: FIRST STEPS TO ACTION

Appreciative Inquiry is about creating connection and space for reflection, as well as about creating new energy, ideas for action, and shared ownership. You can do this by learning while doing, inquiring and experimenting in the day-to-day work. How do you create enough space to experiment? What makes experimenting worthwhile? And what could an experiment look like?

MOVING INTO ACTION: SEVERAL CHANGE INITIATIVES

Most AI processes consist of a lot of conversations: an appreciative interview in pairs, a team meeting that focuses on those aspects of the team in which they excel and the things that sustain their energy, an afternoon in which civil servants enter into conversations with residents and different stakeholders from the city. At a certain moment a shift takes place from conversations about discovering shared strengths and future images, to conversations that create ideas and plans for action. What will we do after today to turn these ideas into a reality? What will I do differently?

Gervase Bushe and Robert Marshak (2014) argue that this transition is one of the crucial moments in a change process and that you need to make sure that you are not looking for the one best solution, but rather that the AI process serves to realize multiple ideas and initiatives for change. This implies that the initiators or leaders do not steer the end result. By inviting participants to connect their own change initiative to the affirmative topic around which the Appreciative Inquiry is centered, a shared responsibility for the results emerges.

WHAT WOULD YOU LIKE TO WORK ON?

To come up with change initiatives or actions, it helps to make the connection with one's personal motivation or drive: Where is your energy at the moment? What would you like to work on? What is really important for you at this moment in time? With these questions everyone can, with the help of colleagues, design collaborative approaches, actions or experiments. Thinking in terms of experiments can help to create space to try out new things. The word experiment in itself already implies that you try out something new and you don't yet know how it will turn out.

In our experience, these are important success factors for working with experiments:

- The experiment is aimed at an issue that is challenging and relevant for the people that are involved in it. There is a feeling of urgency, genuine curiosity, and personal interest to do something about the topic.

- Especially with big problems, which can be daunting and complex, thinking in small steps is vital. A good experiment is therefore small and supports you to do something different the next day, or the next week. By looking for everyday moments in your work that are related to the big issue, you can come up with actionable ideas that in turn will provide clues for working on the main issue in a step-by-step way.

- Thinking and talking about experiments creates reflection. After an experiment you automatically ask yourself how it went, what worked well and what could be better. It is important to capture those moments.

- Thinking in terms of experiments creates safety and space to learn and make mistakes.

- To turn an experiment into a success, it helps to activate the social support system of colleagues in the workplace. For instance, by sharing your experiment with them, doing it together or asking for their help with a specific aspect of the initiative.

A while ago, a number of our colleagues were asked to assist in a change process in a car component factory that had difficulty meeting their quality standards. There was a collective desire to cooperate. People felt a sense of urgency and the quality standards had been discussed several times with operators, line managers and others that were involved. One of the ideas that came out of these conversations was to create a Q-meeting point – a hub where people could talk about quality issues and develop new ideas to enhance product quality. However, not many people visited the Q-meeting point. The initiators asked their colleagues what suggestions they had to improve the meeting point and its operation. To their disappointment, not many colleagues reacted and there were very few ideas. Did this mean that people were not engaged?

They decided to take a step back and enter into a conversation with the operators around the question: What does quality mean to you in your job? In order to facilitate the conversation, the initiators used small picture cards with photos which people could use to speak metaphorically. In no time many images and stories were on the table and the conversation became personal. The second question was: How can *you* influence quality? In this context, people started talking about alertness and reporting mishaps. During the conversation, everyone gradually came to realize that each and every link in the production process – themselves included – could make a difference. This instilled a feeling of responsibility and ownership, not only toward their colleagues, but also toward the clients that would eventually drive the cars for which they produced vital mechanical parts.

The use of pictures evoked a totally different conversation about quality than before. Because it was more personal, people felt part of the conversation. That was triggered because they not only spoke about quality as something that existed outside of themselves, but they also spoke from their own experiences – sharing personal examples and situations. As a result, they began to see their own influence on the broader topic, and conversations evolved from abstract and general statements such as someone should …; management should… or it should be…, to much more personal expressions and ideas: perhaps I can…. After this meeting, thinking of quality-enhancing experiments, in collaboration with the Q-meeting point, was possible.

Looking back, we realized that the idea was initially embraced at a cognitive, but not an *emotional* level. People could see that the quality standards were important, and genuinely cared about quality, but they didn't feel part of the process. By sharing stories and inviting operators to share their curiosity and energy, they began to feel like they were part of the process. This cleared the way for them to step in and start experimenting.

DESIGNING AN EXPERIMENT

We often use (a variation on) the following questions to support people to design their own experiment (Tjepkema, 2010):

- What is the first situation in your work you would want to change?
- How could you design that situation differently?
- What is the smallest thing that you could do differently yourself?
- Who and what do you need to actually do this?

- Who are you going to ask for help?

- With whom are you going to reflect on your experiment and design a next step?

Above all, these questions are meant to keep the experiment small and to ensure that someone feels ownership and a call to action. It is our experience that it works well to express the experiment out loud and to share the plan with colleagues. This makes the step towards starting even smaller and enlists the support of colleagues.

For instance, we recently organized a short workshop in a technical school where the employees thought of a small experiment at the end of the session. The starting question for this group was how they could create more connection between people and a more positive atmosphere in the workplace. Everybody thought of a possible experiment and we ended the session by sharing ideas. Examples included: I want to start with saying Hi to all my colleagues at the first floor when I enter the building every morning, before I disappear into my own room at the third floor. I want to create a space in which we can meet each other as colleagues. We used to have a large picnic table where we met each other at the start of the day, for lunch and during Friday afternoon drinks. We no longer have a meeting place like that. I want to re-create one and I want to practice more of what we have done here today: asking a question before you draw a conclusion.

Half a year later, we were asked to come back for a follow-up workshop to this group. At the start we asked about their experiments: What happened with your ideas? That is such a while back, I have to really think about that, was the most common answer. Or: It is not quite there yet. During lunchtime some employees gave us a tour of the office and we discovered that a lot more had happened than those answers led us to believe. We heard about progress and beginnings: "Here on the first floor we don't see the people who work on other floors that much. Except for Delphine of course, she always starts her day here." Or: "This is the new staff room, we designed and furnished it together a couple of months back, though it is not quite working like we want it to, just five people or so show up here in the mornings..." While walking through the building we came upon some funny motivational posters about the power of questions and curiosity. So, while there were still things to improve in the organization, formulating and sharing an experiment had already made sure that people did some things differently and that a small shift in the desired direction had taken place. Of course, it is very important to make these small steps visible, so that the team can see the progress and build on that.

UNEXPECTED EXPERIMENTS

Do not be surprised when unexpected experiments emerge in a process like this. If you empower people to design an experiment based on what energizes them, some ideas might emerge that you did not see coming. A while ago we worked with a group of operators from a factory. The managing director of the plant expected experiments that would improve the quality of the products or speed up the production process. In the first round, however, people thought of all sorts of initiatives to get to know each other's work better, like a tour in the factory for people who worked in the office and vice versa, and a presentation during lunch time about a new product that was being made in the factory. Despite his initial doubts, the managing director supported all the proposals. In the end it became clear that every single one of the initiatives contributed to more ownership of the product, a better cooperation between the different departments and more commitment within the factory as a whole. In the second round of experiments, partly because those changes, people thought of smart solutions to improve the quality and increase the speed of the production process.

Even though it might appear as if certain experiments will not help to solve the issue directly, it helps to give space to the energy of the experimenters at that moment in time. A while back we worked with a group of people from diverse areas of an organization. Instead of thinking of individual experiments, they thought it was fitting to think of a shared experiment to work on this specific theme. They decided to share an office together for two days a week for the next two months because they came from different departments and did not know each other's work and talents. How this will improve the cross-departmental cooperation in the whole organization? We don't know yet – that is precisely why it is an experiment.

CREATING A SUPPORT STRUCTURE FOR THE EXPERIMENTS

Experiments can help organizations keep discovering and developing, preserve the energy of an AI process and integrate it in the daily work setting. A sort of minimal structure (see also the chapter on orchestrating and improvising) supports this process. For example, sticking with an experiment for forty days (Smit, Pillen & Tjepkema, 2010) or regularly meeting up in experiment groups to reflect on what already works and what can still be improved.

Always start follow-up meetings with anecdotes or an exciting question, to make sure you do not flip into regular meeting or evaluation mode but instead end up in a personal, reflective conversation. Experienced AI facilitators Gervase Bushe and Ron Fry suggest creating an online platform where you can share experiences. Thanks to such a hub (a website, newsletter, or meet-ups) people who are not in the midst of the experiment can also keep track of what is happening which ensures that everyone stays involved and can follow the story while it unfolds.

MAKING SPACE FOR A GOOD CONVERSATION: PLACE MATTERS

At the edge of Square Ledig Erf in Utrecht (The Netherlands) sits a bench that is nearly always occupied by a group of men. Half of them are actually on the bench and the other half uses their parked mobility scooters for seating. Enjoying their habitual cup of coffee or can of beer they discuss the world. People waiting at the bus stop next to the bench are frequently drawn to their conversation, or engage with the men in a short casual exchange. How this bench has become a public meeting space is unknown, but it obviously has.

Organizations have such places, too. Impromptu gatherings occur in the canteen, near the coffee machine, at the secretary's desk and in other physical places. Different types of conversations occur here than at a meeting table or behind a shared desk. If you aim to organize meetings that will generate new ideas and inspirational encounters, then the arrangements for the conversation are important. What questions do we ask? Who sits at the table? The physical location that you choose or set up is just as vital to consider as the questions you ask and the people you invite. How do you literally make *space* for a good conversation?

FIRST, SECOND AND THIRD PLACES

For clarification purposes we will make a brief sidestep into sociology. Ray Oldenburg (1996) is one of the authorities on different types of meeting spaces. He is particularly interested in their societal role and distinguishes between three types:

- The *first place* is the family or home, the safe space in the private setting.
- The *second place* is the professional or work location where business meetings and transactions occur.
- The *third place* is a public meeting space where individuals meet each other away from the home and work domains. Think of: bookshops, cafés, hairdressing salons or the bench at Ledig Erf.

Based on his research, Oldenburg makes a strong case for the importance of *third places* for a community. Places that ensure unity or a spirit of togetherness in the neighborhood, as people from different backgrounds and different generations meet each other and get to know each other in an informal setting. Furthermore, these places are also political and intellectual forums where opinions and ideas are developed and shared, places where opinions are challenged and new thinking may develop. Oldenburg indicates that every district, neighborhood and community needs enough such spaces to survive and be a vibrant, vital place.

Oldenburg's thinking can be applied to organizations as well. Every organization has its third places – and we know that they are important for sharing knowledge and learning. Research from the 1990's into learning on the job featured an important case of a technology firm that, in order to increase productivity halved the space for the canteen. The idea was: if that space were less attractive, staff members would shorten their lunch breaks, leading to more net productive time (Tjepkema, 2003). The decision sparked protest by the workers, who argued that canteen conversations were often about work; they would brainstorm, share knowledge and learn from each other. These conversations often took place with people from different departments or levels in the hierarchy. Responding to this argument, the company decided to transform the freed-up space into formal conference and meeting rooms. However, these were hardly ever used… Conversations that happen in a third place, such as a canteen, cannot be simply transferred to a second space such as a meeting room.

A SPACE FOR ENCOUNTERS AND GOOD CONVERSATIONS

Third place spaces are important, especially when working on learning and innovation because people from different subgroups and cultures can meet each other there. Making meaning of events in an organization, discussing what is worthwhile to sustain or where there is a need for change, does not need to happen only in formally organized forums: the organized get-togethers, presentations, participatory and informative exchange sessions on improvement and innovation. People use informal spaces to engage with each other and it is here that a different type of conversation can emerge – a real addition to the more formal conversations. It works well to look for where these encounters and conversations are currently taking place. What are the equivalents of the third places in your organization? Is there actually a physical space for regular encounters, for instance, at the coffee bar or at the front desk?

What do these spaces look like? Oldenburg identifies several characteristics. First of all, it is a neutral space. This implies that it does not belong to any of those present, so it cannot be a participant's home or office. The space is easily accessible and has a simple or non-pretentious appearance. Status differences play less of a role in such environments, so that you can get to know each other personally. In general, it is a space where people feel at home. The most important activity of the *third place* is talk. The art of conversing and having a good conversation are appreciated here. The conversation is lively, colorful and inviting. Finally, a third place has something magical or playful that draws people in.

LOOK FOR APPROPRIATE VENUES

A possible strategy to start a new, different conversation that moves towards change and innovation is to link up with existing spaces where these informal conversations are being held. Where do groups of employees meet each other? This can be quite a challenge and you might hit it wrong. In a genuine effort to pull their teachers into the conversation on change and innovation in the school, the management team of an educational institution put up posters in staff break rooms. Unfortunately, this initiative backfired. The managers and teachers did not frequent the staff rooms together, so a genuine two-way conversation was not possible. The presence of the posters inadvertently symbolized the distance between the management team and the staff, rather than initiating an informal mutual conversation. What do they want us to discuss this time? We are on our break!

We also came across effective examples. The municipality of a medium sized town wanted to initiate a dialogue with its inhabitants on their community values. The guiding idea was to hold conversations in the square. So, they were planning to invite inhabitants to assemble in the town hall square on a specific Sunday morning for a dialogue on values. Coffee and breakfast would be served to thank people for their participation, but during the initial exploration, doubts crept in. The concern was that such an initiative would only be attractive for limited parts of the population (white, higher educated, aged between 35 and 55, mainly men). So instead, they switched their thinking from the literal meaning of square to the *metaphorical* sense of a meeting place where people gather and asked themselves: Can we identify squares in the municipality that would be attractive to citizens for an inquiry and dialogue on values? They identified five existing lively places, squares, parks, communal centers, where citizens regularly gathered and other stakeholders could be invited to dedicate one of their gatherings to the topic of community values. These gatherings provided for a much richer and more varied dialogue.

CREATING NEW VENUES

The above example was about identifying existing venues. This is not an easy task. In many organizations, similar to society, there are few places where people of different departments or generations meet each other. Generally, employees speak with a limited number of colleagues, and those they talk to are all insiders of the same group. Thijs Homan (2008) calls this "trust groups" or "petri dishes". In his research he discovered that in these small groups meaning and ideas emerge along with a certain shared understanding of situations and developments. Change on a large scale can be enhanced when different groups meet and infect each other with their ideas. To achieve innovation, it helps to organize new encounter spaces where this infection can happen.

To design this process, Homan considers it essential that two conditions are met. Firstly, the groups need to have differing, but not oppositional, points of view. When members of two groups think identically about a certain issue, few new ideas and meanings will arise. If the ideas are totally oppositional, there is the risk of only very limited real exchange, causing, once again, very few new ideas to emerge. It is all about striking the right balance. The second condition is the need for an adequately safe and encouraging environment that is similarly characterized as Oldenburg's third place.

AI *summits* (two day offsite working conferences in which a group goes through all the steps of an AI cycle) often serve the purpose of creating a temporary space where people with different backgrounds can meet each other in person and engage in conversation with each other. This is referred to as, "getting the whole system in the room", like the story of the school that we shared earlier in this book, in which directors, teachers, parents and pupils reflected on the issues of the school during two days.

These AI summits show that it is possible to intentionally create an appropriate venue for a good conversation. In general, this will be a temporary and often a one-off meeting that is organized away from the normal work and meeting places. Oldenburg's design features for third places are a good guide for designing summit spaces.

USING METAPHORS TO INVITE A DIFFERENT WAY OF MEETING

A supplementary way in which to use space to encourage a different type of conversation is to use its symbolic function and its name. We often use language for an encounter or event in organizations that to refers to physical locations: a forum, a market place, a square, a café, a festival, a kitchen table discussion, a workshop, a fire place talk or a laboratory. Using such an image invites people to enter the space with a different mindset and display different behavior than they would in a traditional meeting. A word or metaphor can help people visualize something as a different space. One of the management teams we work with did this successfully by labelling some of their meetings as reflection time, "the kitchen table" and others as decision-time, "the action machine". By these names, they signaled to themselves that different conversations were intended in each meeting. The reflection meetings were more personal, inquisitive and sometimes included guests; employees or a customer. In reality, these were not meetings, but encounters with third-place-like features. The action meetings were more functional, with an agenda and action points; almost a prototype meeting in a second place.

A completely different location can also lead to another type of encounter. How different it is to have a meeting on the neighborhood *in the neighborhood itself*, instead of at the town hall or to have an assessment meeting with a beer in a pub, or to walk on the beach and develop new ideas with your colleague? A carefully chosen place creates an important holding space for your conversations.

THE POWER OF CURIOSITY

A colleague of ours, who works as a civil servant, called one of us while we were writing this book. She was in the process of organizing conversations for a group of junior co-workers, together with other young professionals from her organization. She explained that at some point they asked themselves: Why do young civil servants choose to work for our government? Why did they decide to dedicate their strengths to society? What is that they enjoy in their work? In what type of organization do they really want to work? They had no immediate answers themselves but realized that these were important themes. Their curiosity was the trigger to conduct four group discussions with other young colleagues on these questions. Though that was not the original intent, these conversations eventually enabled them to provide feedback and input to the decision makers in the organization, giving young civil servants a voice.

Her story illustrates how curiosity can foster new initiatives and inquiry. Curiosity is a vital source for development and, in that sense, an important pillar of Appreciative Inquiry processes. Carol Dweck speaks of *the infinite power of curiosity* (Dweck, 2007).

CURIOSITY AND NOT-KNOWING

For years, Suzanne Verdonschot (2015) studied innovation on the work floor. She identified curiosity as an important driver that stimulates people to discover, learn and try out new approaches. Though people may be curious by nature – think of your childhood years and all those things that you discovered or learned out of pure curiosity – as adults at work this proves to be less obvious. According to Verdonschot (2014), the essence of curiosity is a sort of amazement or surprise that drives people to ask questions and to inquire. It is often triggered by a lack of knowledge or a knowledge gap. Leading to questions such as: How does this work? Why can we not succeed in getting this done? Is it possible to...? Might this also work? Curiosity may surface when you find yourself not knowing how things work, because a situation is new to you or it may arise when you have made an error from which you want to learn in order to develop something new or when you have an ambition and goal but are unsure how to go about achieving it.

AN EXPERT CULTURE

With AI, curiosity and not-knowing are explicitly encouraged and combined with a longing for a certain future or ideal. This may catch people by surprise. Organizations are not predominantly set up for wonder, improvisation, learning or inquiry. Their focus is on performance and acting on the basis of what is already known and because this is so deeply embedded in our organizational designs and structures, people start behaving in that way. Think of a team meeting in which colleagues are considered to have formed an opinion on a new proposal and to take a stance on it, rather than to come up with questions. Or, imagine a manager who has to account for disappointing quarterly figures, the question of how this could happen usually serves more as a call to come up with an explanation than as a curious question.

On any working day there can be all sorts of triggers that incite curiosity, but if curiosity or not-knowing is not explicitly appreciated or rewarded, then we will not be inclined to respond in that way. In many organizational cultures, mechanisms prevail that discourage curiosity, such as: rewarding powerful statements, covering up, softening and justification of errors, group pressure to ensure that your behavior and opinions follow the prevalent thinking, and the urgency to quickly make decisions. Many organizations appreciate people with expertise, while at the same time, being seen as an expert implies that people expect you to know the correct answer and to possess the required knowledge and ability. Thinking of, and treating people as experts, does not lead to curious co-workers. "That is outside my realm of expertise", "I know how this works as it is my domain", or "I need to present a good story now as I am responsible", are more typical responses of those with expertise. Curiosity requires a certain tolerance for ambivalence, for admitting to that you do not know something (for the moment) and for acknowledging and accepting that not-knowing (Verdonschot & Spruyt, 2015).

AN EXAMPLE: EXERCISING CURIOSITY FOR A WEEK

To develop a more inquiring atmosphere and attitude with each other, it may help to create a more structured experience of curiosity with staff or colleagues. Together with a large international NGO we came up with an approach to enable colleagues to learn from each other's work in a program that was executed in different countries. In small teams, the colleagues visited other countries for a week. We invited everyone to take on a researcher's role and, as curious colleagues, to look for the hidden qualities of the same program in a different country. In what way was your colleague in that other country exceptional or successful? This approach also served as the *evaluation* of the program.

It turned to be quite a tough job for people to adopt an open mind when viewing each other's work, as they were all experts in poverty reduction, youth engagement and intervention design for social change and justice. It is difficult to ask open questions and adopt an open mind when you are loaded with ideas and assumptions. However, the colleagues in the researcher's role were certainly *not* experts in the context of the country they visited. This helped them adopt a more curious mindset. In addition, we explicitly introduced two outlooks at the beginning of each visit: the expert, who argues from his own experience and work setting, and the inquiring eye or the researcher, who perceives things with an open attitude of not-knowing. Making space for both perceptions worked because the expert viewpoint was allowed to be present. We made an explicit space for it by creating a moment at the end of each day where the visitors could make sense of their observations and experiences. They were invited to analyze what they had witnessed, discern patterns and share their own ideas. This window in time at the end of every day enabled them to maintain the spirit of curiosity the rest of the time.

At the end, one of the most skeptical program directors observed: By experiencing and reflecting with an open mind I have gained a totally new perception of poverty. Now, I even look at poverty in my own country with a different mindset. Turning his inquisitive eye on the country he visited to evaluate the program helped him direct his attention to the situation in his own country differently, enabling him to look afresh at his own working environment.

The example shows that exercising focused curiosity in a new or different context can really fuel inquiry and switch it on for a longer time.

ENCOURAGING CURIOSITY IN THE DAILY WORK PRACTICE

Research into innovation has yielded several general guidelines or tips that are useful if you want to stimulate the curiosity in your group in general, or in the context of the AI-process:

- *Explicitly encouraging and rewarding personal initiative in the domain of inquiry.* Or, as Verdonschot says: When employees, in their annual review, are assessed on what they agreed to do beforehand, and are punished for everything they did outside the agreement, then you can be certain that innovation will be stifled (Verdonschot, 2015). On the other hand, if you discuss whether someone has experimented with new approaches, tried out new things, as something that is expected of them, this will be encouraged.

- *Making space for not-knowing and expressing doubts.* An inquiring attitude, and at times an explicit stance of not-knowing, is essential to arrive at new thinking and solutions. Do you challenge staff members to be open about their doubts and concerns and to make them discussable? Are you open with them about your doubts? Imagine that your team is confronted with disappointing sales figures. In that case you can call on the team with possible solutions. It can also be very effective to do a brainstorm on: What is it that we don't we understand yet? What is surprising or bewildering to us? What are you curious about? I don't have an explanation. I need your help to understand what happened here. You will arrive at other ideas and will acknowledge that not-knowing is permitted or allowed. Curiosity, in its own way, creates the energy to act.

- *Appreciating mistakes and failures.* Mistakes and failures are important drivers of curiosity and of renewal; that one mistake that turned out to be a brilliant discovery or that one product that after two failures turned out to be much improved the third time. We are not talking about mistakes due to negligence, but rather about those that occur because you are trying out something new. These are mistakes that show the limits of your knowledge. How do you respond when a colleague or staff member makes a mistake? What is your first reaction or inclination? What effect does this have on the subsequent handling of mistakes? Are they swept under the carpet or analyzed in detail and shared?

- *Organizing the counter voice.* Inviting somebody with a different way of looking at a situation encourages thinking, avoids tunnel vision and furthermore shows that the contribution of an atypical perspective is appreciated and permitted.

A STRENGTHS-BASED APPROACH

When working with innovative approaches and solutions the inspiration, energy and strengths of the people involved are the most important driver. Likewise, research has shown that people's enthusiasm, innovative capacity, productivity and wellbeing are strengthened when they are able to use their talents to the full in their work (see for instance Schaufeli & Bakker, 2004; Van Woerkom et al, 2010).

Talents and strengths are a common theme in Appreciative Inquiry. We search for people's talents in appreciative interviews, for example, and when inviting people to design experiments we invite them to play to their strengths in their initiatives. Since most people are not very aware of their strengths and talents, a key question is how to get these qualities to the surface: How do you bring these strengths and talents into the limelight? How can you invite people to activate and use their talents optimally, so that by doing so, they develop them even further?

HOW TO DISCOVER TALENTS

There are many definitions of talent floating around. A description that we consider usable and powerful is that of Buckingham and Clifton (2003). They define strengths as *"those behavioral and thought patterns that are natural to us, mostly even unaware"*. Strengths are not so much about skills or competencies; nor are they about excellent performance. They are about what comes naturally to us. For instance, somebody with positivity as a strength will always see opportunities. Someone with a strong action focus takes pleasure in designing and taking the initial next steps: what are we going to do? Someone with ideation is enthused by a brainstorm in which new ideas are developed and so on… It is behavior that comes naturally to you and engaging in activities that play to your strength that energizes you. Of course, there is a relationship between someone's strengths and their skills. What you want and do often is also what you get better at…

Your talent can also be your pitfall. In times of stress, we seek to apply our strengths even more, until we reach a point of ineffectiveness (Dewulf, 2009). Think of the action-focused co-worker who has an angry customer on the phone and immediately starts running around and resolving issues, instead of first exploring what the issue really is, or someone with a sense of responsibility as her strength, who can take on too much and starts having sleepless nights as a consequence. This explains why it is not always possible to identify talents by looking for excellent achievements or asking the question: What are you good at?

A more reliable predictor for someone's strengths is energy. In his more recent work, Buckingham includes this emotional component when speaking of talent. "A strength plays to those activities that make you *feel* strong" (Buckingham, 2007). When somebody drains himself on a certain task, even if he completes it successfully, then it is very likely that he is not applying his natural talents. And the reverse, if somebody leaves a meeting beaming, even though the result was possibly not that great, then it is very likely that person was able to apply his natural strengths – even though it might not be that productive (see Dewulf, 2009). In both cases, work needs to be done and that starts with discovering someone's strengths.

Sitting down with people to explore the question: When are you at your best in your job? often leads to a surprising conversation during which you jointly gain a perspective on their qualities. When were you in flow, achieving good results with lots of energy? Alternatively: When was the last time you went home singing? What did you do that day? What does that tell us about your natural talents?

This sort of conversation has a dual effect; people learn about their talents *and* something happens in the relationship. When people feel seen in their strengths, they feel seen as a person and they tend to apply their strengths more and invite others to deploy their talents, too. That is why it is worthwhile to look at how you would want to organize talent conversations in your organization, either between manager and staff member, amongst coworkers or across teams or departments. Those conversations nearly always have the effect that people start applying their own talents *and* those of others more often.

In one of the teams we coached on strengths, we heard a teacher saying to one of his colleagues: I need to conduct a difficult parental meeting. I am reluctant and scared that my anger will creep in. You have a talent for harmony, so could we do a practice-run to see how I could approach this meeting? The colleague, who received this invitation, was eager to make time for it, as it combined invitation and compliment in one. That is why it is worthwhile to discover talents in a mutual conversation. What are appropriate methods to do so?

AN APPRECIATIVE INTERVIEW ON STRENGTHS

This method starts with a question about a moment or a situation in which somebody felt strong, energized and in flow. You then delve into that story together. What did you do? What qualities did that situation call upon? Mutual insight emerges if colleagues conduct these interviews in pairs.

A pharmaceutical company experimented by applying this approach in their annual performance reviews, with surprising effects. The high performers really needed to sit down and reflect on *how* they had managed to achieve their excellent results. This reflective conversation gave them more peace of mind. If you know how you achieved success, it becomes easier to repeat it. The people who were facing performance difficulties, on the other hand, were also energized. They searched for the positive deviation. When *were* you already (somewhat) successful in this difficult task? What did you do? What strengths did you use? Such questions gave a totally different twist to the conversation and enabled them to explore other possible approaches for the job.

A TEST OR QUESTIONNAIRE

Various self-assessment and reflection tools support the self-exploration of strengths. For instance the book, *Now, Discover Your Strengths*, contains an attractive questionnaire, and on the Internet you can complete the VIA Character Strengths Survey. There are also several books with self-reflection-exercises on talent, such as, *Go with your talent*, developed by Luk Dewulf. It is our experience that these tools are helpful as they present a language and guide reflection. The questionnaires add something to the more obvious open question: What is your talent? People often can only think of what they are good at and they sometimes lack the vocabulary to describe their strengths. Dimensions such as energy and fun, very important indicators of talent are often excluded from people's horizons. Mutual dialogue and exploration of the findings adds value to any self-assessment.

A BIOGRAPHICAL INTERVIEW

The biographical interview has its origins in career coaching. You ask people to look back at their working life and identify moments and periods in which they were exercising their strengths and when they were not. Drawing a history timeline on paper, outlining the highs and lows, makes their strengths highly visible. This helps the person to look back to earlier situations in which they were in their element, or moments in which they climbed out of a low. Those instances are very telling when it comes to a person's strengths. The advantage of this approach is that the context factors quickly become part of the picture. What supporting factors does someone need to flourish in their job? This method is more suited to a personal one-on-one meeting than a group setting.

USE THE ENTIRE GROUP

It is also possible to use the reflections and observations of several team members at the same time, for instance, by making a wall of compliments. During this exercise everyone puts up a sheet of paper with his or her name on it. The team members walk around and jot down the qualities of their team members on their respective sheets. The idea is that everyone writes down something for everyone. Then, people collect the sheet with their name and discuss the inputs in small groups. This leads to inspiring mirrors for people. A bonus is that team members pay more attention to each other's qualities – including the qualities that are at odds with their own strengths. This has a powerful effect on the team's internal group dynamics.

Variations to this method are:

- People use a piece of paper and write about a talent they see in a colleague, then fold the paper and pass it on to the next person. This process continues until everyone has written something. In this way a paper harmonica develops, that at the end can be folded out and studied by its recipient. This is similar to a wall of compliments, the difference being that no-one sees what the others have written.

- Hot seat or a compliment shower: the group sits in a (semi) circle with one person in front. People capture the qualities of their colleague by mentioning them in the group. One member takes notes. After a few minutes, when the group becomes silent, the next person takes his or her turn.

- A patch on the shoulders: people walk round with a packet of post-its. When they have written an identified strength on a post-it for a particular colleague, they stick it on that person's shoulder.

THE CORE: STRENGTHS CONVERSATIONS

Whatever method you choose, the real action is in the interaction. A good conversation on each other's talents is non-judgmental and inquiring. People help each other think and make sense of questions such as: What are your talents? When can you effectively apply this? What would happen if you showed more of this? Or: How can you apply your talents to handle situations that you struggle with?

We observed this closely with a communication agency of a large municipality. They were one manager short and the three remaining leaders were daunted by the performance reviews that needed to be held with almost a hundred communication consultants. How could they give everyone the attention they needed? As an alternative, they conceived an approach in which the team members first worked within their team. Everyone collected feedback from his or her principal clients, and they then discussed the findings with each other, using probing questions to bring about insights. What touched you? What makes you proud? What would you like to improve? In addition, they reviewed each other's talents and strengths. What are your qualities? How would you like to develop them further? Initially people were doubtful about the process, however, as they progressed; everyone began to find these discussions quite exceptional and very inspiring. People who for years had worked on the same team, quite separated from each other with different clients, suddenly discovered very different dimensions of one other through conducting conversations that were about themselves and their development. Informal agreements were made to support each other with specific development points. The management team members were taken by surprise by the quality of the ideas and the energy that people generated in these team conversations. As a result, the managers could hold shorter, but more effective, formal performance reviews. The enormous task that the managers were initially reluctant to handle became the trigger for powerful personal development and improved collaboration in the department.

INTERVIEW: EDDY WILLEMS – SINT-FRANCISCUS COLLEGE
"PEOPLE WHO FEEL RESPECTED, THAT'S THE ESSENCE FOR ME."

Eddy Willems is general director of Sint-Franciscus College (Saint Francis School), a middle and high school of 1650 pupils and 253 staff members in Heusden-Zolder. Central to the vision of the school is: To see the good in young people. To realize that vision in everyday practice, the school has adopted three pillars: close guidance, focus on everyone's talents, and co-creating the school through warm dialogue.

ASKING QUESTIONS SETS A LOT IN MOTION

I apply Appreciative Inquiry in my daily work by making it a permanent feature of the way I deal with people. It simply happens in very small twists that I bring to daily conversations. For example, I mainly pose questions. I notice that it gives people the feeling that they are seen and appreciated, and more so, they get new ideas out of these conversations. For me, those two dimensions are linked; a positive emotion and tapping into potential. Therein lies what I believe to be the essence of AI, elevating people to a higher level by asking the right questions.

My aim is to strengthen and support people's independence and I find that giving appreciation and attention always has an additional effect: people start to behave in a more positive way. It's essential that I don't ask questions as a way to get something – it's not a transaction. For me, it's all about making people feel good and respected. That's the core. If you focus too much on the usefulness, it becomes a transparent trick. My starting point is the conviction that positive emotions are the driver for develop potential and that's where the good things come from.

BASIC VALUES

For me, this is all closely related to our pedagogical project at school. We believe in the good of people and that everyone deserves respect. When you give pupils and staff the feeling that you strongly believe in them, they will grow and their best selves will emerge. I link this with the pillars of the school's vision and the values of Saint Francis, whose name we carry; respect, service, solidarity and trust. These values are inspirational for me, and I try to live up to them in my way of living and working with others.

THE APPRECIATIVE EYE

Of course, at times this is difficult, and it really feels like a conscious personal choice to take this perspective. Sometimes I find myself disappointed by the results. In such cases, I deliberately put on my positive glasses to look for what they have done well, what their intentions were, and how I can both voice my disappointment and tap into their strengths and positive intentions in the conversation. I strongly believe that we have to keep emotional wellbeing as our principal aim. There simply is no other way. Consider the alternative, in which we would phrase things succinctly in a negative way, leaving people numb and down. You would have to pour much energy into building their strength up again. Compared to that, maintaining an appreciative eye takes little effort so it appears to suit me well. There was a time that I thought choosing this approach was because I was hesitant to phrase things in a negative way. I now know that is not the case. I do not shy away from anything.

AI WAS FAMILIAR TO ME – AND NEW AT THE SAME TIME

The first time I learned about AI was in a session with our board of directors. For me it was a strong affirmation of what I was doing and at the same time it was an eye opener. Suddenly I saw possibilities of applying it systematically and consciously. The link with other processes that I did not yet approach in this manner became obvious to me. Suddenly, there were so many new possibilities.

We have used AI in many ways within our school. For instance, recently we took two days to think about the future of our institution. The reason was that we will move from two separate locations to one joint campus. In the history of the school this is a very important event and it provides an excellent opportunity to think about the pillars on which the school is built and to clarify our vision for the future. Instead of developing this in the boardroom we decided to bring all stakeholders together for two days; our pupils, teachers, pupil mentors, parents, directors and board. Since our ambition is to be a true warm dialogue school, we needed to move beyond giving people a voice. We also had to bring them into the decision making at every level. The shared experience was very positive and the outcome much better than we had hoped for.

EVEN MORE OPPORTUNITIES

I can see many opportunities for our school to do more with Appreciative Inquiry. My ultimate wish is that it becomes the conscious basic attitude for every teacher to see the best in every pupil. Especially for those who have not travelled an easy route in life, challenging them in a positive way and working towards their emotional well-being is crucial. By showing AI as a way of life, I hope to inspire the teaching staff to follow suit and to attempt to do the same. This approach is linked to my ideal of the warm dialogue school; to give everyone the feeling of being welcome, to continue the dialogue, and to ask the questions that energize everybody. I can still see several AI-seeds that I would like to plant in St Francis School.

WHAT DOES AI ASK OF YOU AS A MANAGER?

AN APPRECIATIVE EYE

Japanese artist Shigeo Fukuda (1932 – 2009) was a master of illusions. His installation, Underground Piano, is a delightful and intriguing example. As a spectator, if you approach the work of art from the right side you see components of a grand piano, apparently arranged in a haphazard fashion. If you stand on the left, however, there is a mirror. From a specific angle, the mirrored image forms a perfect grand piano.

Somehow, and for us at least, this artwork displays the essence of the AI perspective. At the core of Appreciative Inquiry is a choice in your perspective. Reality has multiple sides, multiple faces. There is not one definition or absolute truth. To a degree the question then becomes: Which perspective do we choose?

AI has a methodological side, and to an extent that is what this book is about; creating history timelines, organizing dream sessions with colleagues, and conducting appreciative interviews. These are all helpful practical building blocks. However, AI is first and foremost a change philosophy. The way in which you approach an issue or question from this perspective has a number of fundamental characteristics that we describe as Appreciative Inquiry which manifest themselves in a different approach.

Without such a perspective the AI working methods lose their power, or worse, they are effectively turned into simple tricks. The genuine application of AI starts with the way you perceive. It is a basic attitude with which to approach development, people and collaboration. It is not simply naïve optimism, focusing only on what goes well and closing your eyes for what doesn't work. But what *is* it then?

THE APPRECIATIVE EYE

Appreciative Inquiry starts with the realization that we can determine for ourselves how we look at the world around us, every day. It is easy and perhaps therefore seductive to see illustrations of what is wrong and what does not function well. Brain research shows that our brain responds more strongly to negative deviations, to what does not go as we had expected or what does not perform as planned. Intuitively, we react to signals that seem to signify scarcity or danger (Zander & Zander, 2002). The one low mark on the school report of your child will catch your eye sooner than the higher ones. The one dissatisfied customer who calls to voice his complaints, will be more top-of-mind to the sales crew then all the people who – often without speaking out – were happy clients.

Simply put, we continuously receive implicit invitations to see problems and to resolve these. What does it mean to view the world differently, to look with an appreciating eye? It certainly doesn't imply wearing rose-colored glasses that give a naïve perception of the world and events. Rather it is about adopting the belief that both we and our environment changes in the direction of that what we give attention to. David Cooperrider calls this the appreciative eye (e.g. Cooperrider & Whitney, 2005). Are we capable of approaching ourselves and the world around us with the intention of seeing what strengths are already present, and asking ourselves how we might use these for the development towards a future that we would like to become reality?

OUR OUTLOOK DETERMINES WHAT WE SEE

The significance of the choice for our perspective has been documented in the well-known research into the Pygmalion-effect (Rosenthal & Jacobson, 1968). When we have high expectations of people, their performance improves, and vice versa. The research setting for this study was a mathematics teacher's new class of pupils. At the beginning he was told what type of pupils he had in his class. Based on (fabricated) test results he was informed that the class could be divided in two groups. One group of pupils, who in the past year had high scores for mathematics and displayed a strong drive for achievement in the subject and a second group of pupils who had lower results in mathematics and a significantly lower achievement drive. The teacher was informed in detail which pupils belonged to which group. In reality, there was no difference between the groups in achieved results or motivation. Better and slower pupils had been spread evenly over the two groups. But in the teacher's mind, one group of pupils was better and more motivated than the other. After some time, the test results of the pupils from the so-called better group were significantly higher than the results from the second group, even though, at the beginning of the term there was no difference in mathematics ability between the two groups.

Teachers strongly criticized the findings and experienced them as an attack on their professionalism. They felt wrongly accused of treating pupils differently and discriminating amongst them. However, researchers repeated the Pygmalion research in different places with even stricter research conditions. Each time, their findings confirmed the initial results. What was remarkable in the teacher's behavior was that when a "good" pupil gave a correct answer, the teacher confirmed his perception by the way he reacted. An incorrect answer of the same pupil was regarded as an exception: Oh dear, you have made mistake. Or: Next time you'll succeed. The behavior towards "weaker" pupils was exactly the opposite; the reaction to incorrect answers displayed a confirmation of the prevalent image held by the teacher – as if she or he had expected it, and correct answers were seen as a stroke of luck.

PYGMALION ON THE WORK FLOOR

When translating these findings to an organizational setting, a similar phenomenon can be found. Staff members that have a reputation of being a good colleague are easily forgiven for an error or a critical remark. Whereas staff members with a poor reputation can perform well nine times and yet attract a lot of criticism for a mistake during the tenth effort. Plans that we have faith in are given a second chance, while plans that we have doubts about are withdrawn at the first setback. Teams that we believe in receive positive attention and new opportunities, while teams that are seen to be blemished often struggle and find it hard to break the negative cycle. As human beings, we are subconsciously inclined to seek confirmation of our existing idea of reality, *even if* that reality has different facets, layers and faces, and cannot be reduced to one single universal truth.

Could change then start by altering our idea of reality? Or at least with the realization that we can choose what to focus on, and that this choice will influence at least partly what will unfold. Similar to the way Fukuda invites us to look in a specific manner and then determine what we see: a pile of rubbish or a piano? In his book *Appreciative Intelligence*, Tojo Thatchenkery (2006) sees this as a capacity; he advocates that people can train their eye to see the potential in situations and people.

POSSIBILISM

This is not about naïve optimism. A participant in one of our AI learning networks phrased it as: "An optimist has the inclination to somewhat naively push problems away. Problems are minimalized or ignored. A pessimist disguises himself as being analytical and realistic. He is very apt to see problems and then pitches that these are the simple facts and that we have to come to terms with their existence. Neither of them is starting from a whole perspective. There is a third choice, that of the possibilist. A possibilist acknowledges problems and sees possibilities. Problems are there, but he shifts the focus to the desire and hope behind the problem." Every problem is an opportunity to shift the attention from the unwanted past to the desired future.

Hope or hopelessness? Both are often present. The perspective that we choose influences the direction we evolve towards. It is not about ignoring or downplaying problems, it is rather about appreciating, in the sense of acknowledging that problems are present and approaching them from the question of what we have going for us to resolve them, to build on what is already there, to look for usable assets and ways forward. In 2014, Alice Herz-Sommer passed away. She was 110 years old and at the time of her death she was the oldest survivor of the holocaust. During the Second World War she had been imprisoned in a concentration camp. Following these dreadful times, she managed to restart her career as a concert pianist and achieve renewed fame and success. In a remarkable documentary on her life, she was 109 years old at the time, the interviewer inquired into her secret. How has she managed to age so healthy and successfully? She answered by explaining her way of perceiving life and the world, "I know about the bad, and I choose to look for the good. Everywhere you look, there is beauty." A truly remarkable and impressive statement about a determined personal choice, all the more so, because of her life's story (Rusbridger, 2006).

COURAGE AND A SENSE OF REALITY

Does it take courage to choose to look at life this way, to see opportunities and potential, and to focus on those even in situations where negative issues are fighting for your attention? According to the philosopher and leadership expert, Peter Koestenbaum, an essential leadership quality is the capacity to deal with these types of polarities and dilemmas. His proposition is that as human beings, we are always free to choose how we look at things and what we focus on. What may often hold us back in making a choice are the tensions that a decision might entail. His proposition is that it is important to recognize that tension, and to actually explore it and deal with it. By getting the dilemma out in the open and consciously investigating how best to deal with it, authentic and deliberate choices can be made rather than choices driven by fear, for instance.

According to Koestenbaum, strong leaders know how to deal with four dimensions:

- Reality: see the reality as it is, not as you would like it to be. Look at the facts in a no-nonsense manner.

- Ethics: be value driven, based on principles, honesty and integrity.

- Vision: remain in contact with what is possible, based on images of what is feasible combined with the expression of your desires and wishes.

- Courage: realize that you are free to act, to stand up and go forward, you have the capacity to make things happen because you have chosen to do so.

In his approach, leadership requires the integration of these four dimensions, knowing that at times they can be fundamentally in opposition with one another. Courage ensures that the other is possible, that you can make a choice at any moment in time. Greatness comes with recognizing that your potential is limited only by how you choose, that is, how you choose your freedom (Koestenbaum, 2002).

This makes it a personal matter. Adopting an appreciative eye is not a feature that is reserved for people who happen to possess an optimistic character. Rather, it can be a conscious choice for anyone to adopt a certain perspective. Several of the leaders we interviewed for this book refer to this choice. They talk about how they maintain an appreciative eye for opportunities, potential and possibilities even when they are facing poor results, or other headwinds. They stress that this is a choice they make not at one point in time, but again and again because they value what this perspective brings and/or because they do not feel at home with the alternative.

A NOT-KNOWING STANCE

Besides an appreciative eye, an inquiring attitude is an essential component of the Appreciative Inquiry perspective. By asking questions that generate energy, elicit new ideas and focus the attention on where you want to go you can encourage movement and change. The way in which you ask your questions is important. People sense when questions are inviting and truly focused on inquiry and dialogue. Authenticity counts. So, how can you put your curiosity in the lead?

As a leader, a not-knowing, questioning stance is not always an obvious approach. There is something about our organizational culture that implicitly makes managers expect themselves to have the answers. Moreover, others expect it too – even while grumbling about it. Independent of who you are as a person, this attribute belongs to your role, so it seems. In addition, it seems that managers are primarily selected for their capacity to make decisions, to carry responsibility, to achieve results, to be knowledgeable and to *act*. These traits are in many ways very valuable strengths. However, if you want to get started with Appreciative Inquiry, such expectations can also be quite a challenge. Can you find the space and time to seek and identify the question that will help create movement? Are you able to engage in conversations, even though it might feel as if these conversations initially only slow things down?

As a manager, embarking on a change process with questions, rather than answers, is not always an obvious strategy, because the asking of questions implies more than simply sharing information. Involving people is a matter of sharing responsibility –that is its strength (Marquardt, 2004). It is essentially a different management style than more conventional approaches.

LETTING GO AND TRUSTING

We worked with a factory director, Marcel, who had consciously chosen to work with Appreciative Inquiry because he wanted to experiment with a new management approach. In a number of ways his story illustrates what it takes to adopt an AI approach in a management position.

Marcel was an experienced leader who had managed to improve several factories in his career, each starting from dire circumstances. He had always thought of the interventions himself: readjusting machinery, rearranging production paths, improving work processes. This had always led to quick and even surprising gains, but he nevertheless faced a sense of ambiguity and even dissatisfaction. A persistent question nagged in the back of his mind: How long would the change last? What real difference had his changes made for the company and the people employed? Were the results a temporary success or were the people involved now able to respond to new challenges?

At one point, Marcel took on a new job to revive a company in trouble. Only this time, he was determined to approach the necessary change process in a different manner. He wanted to work bottom-up, establishing an active role for the operators, engineers, salespersons and the team leaders. He was keen to use their knowledge and drive, so that they too would learn about the factory and its operations. Furthermore, he wanted them to feel genuinely valued. Appreciative Inquiry appeared to him to fit the bill.

His initial choice for this way of working was cognitive and rational. Very quickly it dawned on him that this approach was not only technical, but also demanded courage and confidence, even called on an emotional commitment. The plant was part of a multinational concern with a strong focus on shareholder profits. Every quarter Marcel would board the plane to go to the company's HQ for a meeting on the quarterly figures of his factory. Initially, these did not show much improvement, which increased the pressure put on him. Meanwhile, he was hard at work in the factory, working with the operators and team leaders, setting up a variety of appreciative interviews and experiments. However, the first two quarters the hard work in the factory did not lead to apparent and obvious results. It took a lot of effort and courage for Marcel to continue inquiring and to withstand his inclination to take over and provide direction to the staff. Even more so, as the operators started with experiments that he did not immediately recognize as particularly useful or effective – he considered them to be too careful. He would have done it differently. At times he would stand in front of his office window, that provided him with an excellent view on the production floor, and wish he could be in control.

What motivated him to stay his course was that, even though he did not see the effects immediately in the spreadsheets and dashboards, he could see that the behavior of the operators started to change. They demonstrated more responsibility, were more enthusiastic and started looking for each other's company. This observation touched him, made him enthusiastic and gave him confidence to persist and withstand the pressure for quick results from HQ. When, towards the end of the year, the hard figures showed positive increases, it was quite a relief to Marcel. Now, three years later, the profitability of the factory has increased consistently– as have the indicators for product quality and staff engagement, and this has made both directors and staff proud.

Changing by asking questions requires managers to let go, to trust that an answer will come even though that could well be a different answer from the one you anticipated. Marcel really needed to let go of his ideas on how the factory should operate and work with the ideas that came from the work floor. Asking questions can make it possible for you to confront your own knowing and not-knowing, your assumptions and implicit ideas. Often, things turn out differently from what you had assumed. Michael Marquardt sees this as the main task for managers in a change process. We have to have willingness and courage to practice not knowing. Change requires challenging and letting go of old convictions and patterns – including your own – so that something new can emerge.

BEING OPEN AND EAGER TO KNOW

This is all related to the next challenge. Asking the right questions is one thing. The way in which you ask the questions is just as important, especially when you as a manager pose questions to a subordinate or direct report. The position you have and the way you ask your questions influences how they are received. "Depending on how the leader asks the question, they can be perceived as an invitation, a request, or a missile." explains researcher Goldberg (in Marquardt, 2004).

When a question is suggestive, or you know the answer already, or you are very keen for a certain type of answer, it will likely not have the desired effect. Appreciative Inquiry only works if you genuinely want to understand, to discover something new. It challenges you to face your not-knowing as a space for curiosity.

Marcel, the factory director in our example initially started with the question: How can we increase the on-time delivery? In other words, how can we ensure that our products are delivered to our clients on time? He had his own ideas but was also genuinely curious to find out what the group would propose. At first, the operators and engineers were a little hesitant: Does he really mean this? Can we say whatever we think or is there a correct answer? Has he got something in mind already? Will all our ideas be included? The fact that the previous manager had for years applied a directive management style played a significant role – a new chief executive who asked questions was a fundamental shift in style, one that people in the factory needed to get used to. It took a while, and persistence on the part of Marcel, to get into an open dialogue.

EXPERIMENTING WITH YOUR QUESTIONS

There is no golden rule that will ensure that your question is understood as an invitation. There are suggestions and ideas, but the most important factor, besides your genuine curiosity, is practice. Posing questions that set something in motion is not something that you learn and practice at school, in leadership training, or at work. How often do you ask, or receive, feedback on the questions that you pose, so that you can learn their effect? Something that you do not practice, will likely not improve. Trying out different questions and seriously exploring their effect will help you to hone this skill. Not giving up too easily helps as well. Or as a director of marketing voiced it, "At the beginning I experienced the asking of questions as uncomfortable and frustrating. I struggled to pose the right questions. At times I asked suggestive or closed questions or I only asked questions when I knew that I needed to make a decision. I only invited defensive behavior."

The only way you can change this is by improving your understanding on how your questions are received, both in the specific situation that you are in and with those people that you are working with. Because your colleagues and staff might have to get used to it as well, a new way of conversing is something that you can only develop together – questioning and searching, probing and scanning.

This kind of experimenting is part and parcel of the courage needed by a manager to engage in an Appreciative Inquiry change process. Marquardt explains it as: "You can't think yourself into courage; you can only act yourself into courage" (2011). Obviously, you will only engage in this practice if what is to be gained exceeds the potential hurdles you perceive. As in the case of Marcel, for whom the real reward was that the group of operators felt more committed, gave more of themselves, and had the feeling that they truly mattered. All of which was – besides the operational results – vital for the survival of the factory.

ENCOURAGEMENT: THE POWER OF PRESENCE

Appreciative Inquiry conversations typically mobilize energy, enthusiasm and practical ideas for improvements. People leave these conversations with energy and positive intentions. How can you maintain this in a way that the ownership remains with the participants and that you maintain the collaborative momentum? How can you foster and facilitate continued collaboration without taking over, implementing, securing or containing ideas to project plans? Is it possible to be a change facilitator and a coach, in your role as manager?

Gervase Bushe and Ron Fry gave a clear answer during the WAIC 2012: "Once you have started the fire, keep on encouraging initiatives and give the fire some oxygen." From their review of successful AI processes, it became apparent that encouraging and following up on AI initiatives by leadership is more effective than the more traditional project management. Bushe and Fry call this *tracking & fanning*; following and encouraging. Why does it work so well? And how might you do this yourself?

AN INFRASTRUCTURE FOR EXPERIMENTS

The starting point is to ensure that ideas rapidly lead to real action – a first move, even a small one. General intentions are difficult to turn into concrete actions. In our experience, an effective first move is the design of an experiment in the sense of a rapid, visible action. Creating an infrastructure which allows everyone to capture and follow these experiments provides structure. Fry and Bushe call this creating a hub. For example, a regular meeting of experimenting groups, or physically collecting the stories of experiments on a website or making posters allows you to track what is going on... Celebrating the harvest by making it visible and reflecting on what worked in an experiment, what the next step could be, what people want to see more of – fans the fire.

PROGRESS IS MOTIVATING

A study conducted by Teresa Amabile and Steven Kramer (2012) sheds light on the importance of this active and noticeable monitoring of progress.

They conducted journal research with staff on the questions: What provides energy in work? What motivates people to give the best they have? One common theme emerged from the thousands of journal entries from people in very different organizations; chemical industry, services, manufacturing, and found that making progress on a meaningful task is motivating for everyone. They called this *the progress principle*. When people have the feeling that they can take a project a step forward, finalize an action point, or help somebody else progress, they are energized to continue. The reverse can also be the case. When projects are suddenly stopped, client satisfaction figures are disappointing. When collaboration on a task gets stuck in difficult conversations, energy levels drop. As we have noted earlier, both realities may exist simultaneously in any project or initiative. The key is the choice you make to focus attention on progress being made or the lack of it. After all, we move in the direction of what we most frequently ask questions about.

This sounds easier than it is in practice. In general, we are not always sufficiently aware of the importance of sensing or intentionally attending to progress. Amabile and Kramer asked people to name five concepts that were important to motivation, such as rewards and recognition, in order of priority. Only five percent of the managers and employees put making progress at the top of the list, while the journals showed that this was the most important motivational source. We seem to have a blind spot for the importance of the feeling of making progress.

SOMETIMES, WE STOP TOO SOON

Even when we do make progress, the pressures of daily practice can involve so many factors that they prevent people from seeing and valuing that progress. For example, think of a team of front desk receptionists who, after an AI-brainstorm with colleagues, optimistically make adjustments to improve the guest experience. In daily practice, they are still confronted with dissatisfied people and complaints. What do they focus on? Or consider the improvement team that successfully addresses four different bottlenecks in the production line, but after a month does not yet reach their target of eight, consequently leaving the dashboard for this section in red. How can they still value their progress?

Because of these kinds of disappointing experiences, people often stop experimenting with new behavior. Many behavioral changes simply get stuck in the phase of good ideas, even if it was a person's own idea that was important to them and they began brimming with energy. Realizing true change, demands repeated experimenting, self-encouragement and learning from what is succeeding. Adopting new behavior with each other is a tough job. How can you support people to sustain this?

ENCOURAGEMENT

In our experience, the following elements are encouraging for people in developing new behavior:

- Identification and capturing progress steps, no matter how small. Sometimes it is easier for an outsider to identify progress than for the people involved. For instance, the front desk staff, who still receive complaints, but also now have a larger number of satisfied customers or the improvement team that managed to deal with bottlenecks. The achievement is not yet conclusive, but there are significant steps in the right direction and it helps to identify these (Smit, Pillen & Tjepkema, 2010). Asking about this progress is very powerful – and makes people see it for themselves (Amabile & Kramer, 2012).

- Positive feedback; providing information on what works. Giving a compliment for what you see somebody do and identifying the impact of their action. This is different from a general remark such as: Well done! What works for people is *precise* information on what they did and the positive impact (Smit, Pillen & Tjepkema, 2010). A complimentary question might also work: How did you manage to achieve that? And pursuing that inquiry to really uncover what made it possible. Simply paying attention to someone's intention and contribution can have a positive effect. It is all about making the progress visible.

What also helps is:

- Design a next step together. To make progress, it is essential to continue making progress. It is important that the engine keeps running and that someone experiences the new behavior and its effect. No success without success experiences... Thinking along with someone on what a logical next step could be, can be a very powerful intervention. For example, with the question: How would you like to experiment with this afresh tomorrow? Perhaps you also want to join the brainstorm, suggesting ideas. As long as it is not perceived as telling someone what to do, this type of management behavior is seen as motivating by employees (Amabile & Kramer, 2012).

You can support others to turn their own discoveries and ambitions into action by helping them design small, but meaningful experiments and to subsequently notice the progress made, give positive feedback and assist with the design of next steps toward improvement.

CREATING FOCUS BY SETTING CRITERIA

When we ask managers what characteristic they would most appreciate seeing amongst their colleagues and staff members, the answers are often related to themes of engagement and ownership. Leaders really want people to feel involved and engaged around a topic, their team and the organization they are part of. The quickest way to achieve involvement is literally by involving people. You may do this because you genuinely feel their vision and experience are needed, because you sense that you are not able to answer a particular question from your own knowledge and background alone or simply because you like to create together with others.

However, if you phrase the invitation to be involved in a general fashion, it hardly works. Inviting a team to provide input or to share their thoughts with you doesn't automatically lead to a response. The CEO of a bank opened an idea-box with this invitation: If you have an idea on how to improve the bank, email me. To his disappointment, he got only a few messages. Did this mean that staff in the bank was completely satisfied? Did they lack ideas? Neither was the case. Experience shows that people need something more to become involved and to share their thinking. First of all, a clear topic or question, so that people feel invited to input to something important, valuable, or strategic. Such a focused invitation produces significantly more responses, in our experience. Getting people to step in with their ideas and voices requires that you provide direction and focus. The question is: How do you do that without boxing things in?

HOW TO KEEP INPUT MANAGEABLE?

How do we involve staff members? was the question posed by the board of directors of a care institution for mentally challenged children and adults. The care environment was going through major shifts and the board saw the need to (re-)position the organization and to prepare themselves to face the future. Boardroom discussions on the strengths of the organization and their personal dreams and ambitions for the future had been connective and profound. They realized that it brought them to themes and questions that they wanted to explore with a wider group of stakeholders; clients, family members of clients, staff members, partner organizations and government.

The quality and engagement they had experienced in their own conversations provided them with the confidence that conversations with a wider group of participants would also work.

At the same time there were concerns. If we involve others, how can we keep this manageable? By this, they really meant: Can we do justice to all the energy and ideas that will arise? The question of manageability highlights an interesting dilemma; on the one hand we are keen to involve others and realize how essential this is, and on the other hand we want to be assured that we can progress with all the received input. We do not want to end up in endless collective searches for consensus, nor do we want to create misguided expectations amongst people.

A RIVER WITHOUT BANKS IS JUST A SWAMP

Using criteria is a productive way of addressing the manageability dilemma, as these provide room and clarify the boundaries – or guardrails – for collaborative thinking. Criteria are the bridge between the strategic window that looks at the higher-level ambition or final result, and the practical window of operational solutions. Working with criteria mediates the extremes: planning and control, or letting a thousand flowers bloom. A question that helps to define criteria is: Would you as management agree with every idea or every proposal?

Generally, the answer is negative. So, the subsequent question is: What should a good idea consist of? The answers to that question are the criteria that can be used to assess the proposed ideas or solutions. In turn, these can be used to channel the energy and make the stream of ideas productive.

In the case of the care institution mentioned above, the effect of asking these two questions was twofold. Firstly, the board had the feeling that their question on manageability was acknowledged. Secondly, the questions invited them to jointly identify five criteria. Ideas and proposals should be:

- Aligned with the core theme of our inquiry. In other words, contributions need to be relevant and contribute to the realization of ambitions that are contained in our core theme.

- Actionable and provide guidance to the necessary steps that need to be taken. Note that this is different from being *immediately* actionable. We want to also give space to ideas that could produce results in the long term. As long as the idea of implementation can be seen at the horizon.

- Within our own sphere of influence. Proposals that make us dependent on others have limited value.

- Supporting us to prepare for the changing policy framework that is being formulated by the government.

- Building on the values and vision of the organization.

The board perceived that these criteria answered their concern for a manageable participatory process. Every idea or proposal that answered these criteria could be welcomed and supported. The result of this conversation was a board that could enter the group conversations with confidence and curiosity for what could become possible.

SHARED RESPONSIBILITY FOR THE CRITERIA

Whenever we involve others in a participatory process, it becomes important to make the criteria explicit. In an AI-process this is best done after the Dream phase, at a time that you are about to start designing, since this allows participants to first have the opportunity to think beyond the (assumed) boundaries of the desired future. At the transition from Dream to Design phase the criteria can easily be put on the table. It is even possible to involve participants in formulating or fine tuning these criteria. With that, you invite people to take joint responsibility and avoid senior leadership being forced into a solitary position of being the criteria guardian. Although it is inevitable that they have this role, it is worthwhile to share that responsibility with the whole group when designing ideas and proposals. In this way, individual responsibility becomes shared responsibility.

MAKING SPACE FOR INQUIRY

A work setting is usually not set up for inquiry. We are generally geared towards informing, producing, deciding, resolving and doing, both in a practical and a intellectual sense. Both our conversations and meetings are implicitly focused on drawing conclusions as quickly as possible. Appreciative Inquiry calls on you to make space for reflecting, inquiring, brainstorming and playing in many ways. This is more than just a question of methods and methodologies, it also relates to your attitude and focus as manager. Appreciative Inquiry asks for space in several dimensions.

Space refers to the need for *location and time*, moments when you are able to be in dialogue with each other, to experiment and to reflect. This is essential and not always easy to find or create. Fortunately, experience tells us that you can have considerable progress in a short period. Recently, an organization convened an AI conversation with over four hundred people in a gathering that only took two hours. This was a very productive encounter. A smart design with a focus on meaningful questions can ensure that time is used efficiently. It does however require you to create such a space.

AI also calls for *mental space*. The philosopher Jos Kessels (2002) writes about free space, referring to the initial meaning of the Greek word of *skolè* – school. He refers to a space to think and to engage in philosophical thought, but also to play and to experiment. How can you create such a space in a work context? The questions we pose in an AI-process are important here. You consciously look for expansive and unusual questions that invite people to move beyond existing boundaries. What are your dreams? What do you want to expand? Where are you already successful? What are your sources of energy? By dreaming and constructing a prototype you play with ideas of the future. Obviously, besides the methodological aspects, your attitude as a manager has great influence. Are you open to inquiry? Or are you impatient and eager to shift immediately into action mode?

Finally, *relational* space is needed, wherein you can truly engage with the questions and embark on inquiry. Where everything is allowed to exist: counter-voices, concerns, and the I-don't-know-yet. This is where there is some space to play and to try things out. As manager or process facilitator you play an important role with the way you position yourself. At times it might appear that you are not making a significant contribution. The reverse is true. You might not be actively involved in the conversation, but you are creating and holding the space, and this is what we will explore below.

CONTAINMENT: HOLDING SPACE

Learning and development can evoke insecurity and stress as you first have to go through a phase of not-knowing, abandoning existing beliefs, entering a state of confusion as your idea of the issue is confronted with other viewpoints that appear to be at least equally true. That confusion and not-knowing is functional, because only then will new ways of inquiring and seeing emerge. We have to leave our *comfort zone* for the *zone of proximal development* where there is something undeniably adventurous and energizing, but there is also an obvious tension. In that respect, *containment* is important. According to Yvonne Burger and Arnold Roos (2012), what is essential in containment is to avoid short-changing, fleeing or adopting another form of defensive behavior. People must dare to engage with the challenges that lie ahead. The question is how you create a setting in which participants can withstand that tension in such a way that space for development emerges.

This suggests that it is essential to give space for insecurities and fears, to neutralize them, so that they may be present and at the same time not obstruct the conversation and thought process. Another word for this is *a safe space*. As the facilitator or manager, you can act as a buffer for negative feelings. Burger and Roos (2012) explain this eloquently. The feelings of insecurity and fear are projected onto the manager and are accommodated and translated so that staff members can focus on their primary task. In this case that task is the appreciative inquiry or the experimenting. In practical terms, that containment role is developed when the facilitator recognizes feelings of fear, articulates these, and reassures that they are ok, so these feelings can continue to exist and at the same time be palatable for the group.

Otto, chairman of the Board for a large educational institution, started an exciting conversation with the school's entire management, focusing on the collaboration between Board and management. This was a hot topic as the collaboration was not optimal at the time. An Appreciative Inquiry approach was chosen to learn how to improve. The outcome of the exchange was very positive, partly due to the role that Otto took. He said the least of all those present but did invite everyone to express themselves. During the conversation he calmly responded to everything that was said, including (or especially) when besides wishes, issues were raised that people felt were problematic. In particular, he expressed non-verbally that such feelings were acceptable. It might have appeared that he was doing nothing, but as he sat at the head of the table, he kept the space intact so that others could speak out, think out loud and explore what they would like to work on with each other.

Presence from the facilitator or leader is a powerful factor. To be there attentively and calmly is essential. When you are in a hurry or not fully present, experience a lot of pressure, are opinionated or irritated, it will be difficult to achieve containment. The more you are aware of your containment role, the stronger it will be.

Two final remarks regarding the topic of your attention and providing a holding space:

- Paying attention to the physical setting and set-up is important. A location where you can be at ease or even at some distance from the daily work practice has impact. Practical things such as maintaining clear and feasible start and end times may prevent an irregular in- and out-flux which could disrupt good conversation. The arrangement of the room, the methods you use... may serve to help a group contain emotions associated with challenging aspects of changing.

- Keeping an eye on the whole person and not just the official role also contributes to an environment where people will dare to explore challenges and feelings of unease and deal with them. This may involve attention for someone's personal situation if needed.

In the sections of this book dealing with tools and techniques, we elaborate on the more methodological aspects of these issues.

LISTENING ATTENTIVELY

Asking questions and the capacity to really listen to the other are closely linked. How can you listen to what the other has to say in such a way that the other really feels heard? How can you hear what is happening in the organization?

It seems so obvious; listening to the other, being attentive to what's happening – and still we all know that this is not self-evident. Remember that meeting during which you found your mind wandering to all those other chores that you still needed to do that day or that moment when you found out that something had been brewing in the organization or in your team and, in hindsight, you realized that you had been too preoccupied to notice this, or the conversation during which staff members enthusiastically shared some new ideas – and you realized that they interfered with your own plan. How do you continue listening?

During a leadership development program, Roald gradually realized that one of his most significant development themes was being able to pay more attention to others. Following an afternoon outdoors in nature, this realization really hit home. "For me it is very difficult to be attentive. Both in my private life and at work I struggle to be truly engaged in conversation. I *want* to change that... I will also *need* that to be more impactful." He decided to work on his ability to be fully present, and to listen. Enthusiastically, he engaged himself in experimental conversations with staff members and colleagues only to find that he still found it difficult to really change his listening skills. What was going on? And what would help him?

LISTENING AS THE KEY TO A GOOD CONVERSATION

Why is it so important to listen with full attention to the other? We think of listening as receiving what is being said, but also being attuned to the manner of speech, the intonation, the body language, and what is not being said aloud. In this context, the British philosopher Richard Sennett quotes a famous lawyer who once said, "People who do not observe, cannot converse." According to Sennett (2013) listening has to do with the way in which you establish connection and respond to the meaning you make with each other. Following attentively, interpreting and making sense of what the other says before you give an answer. It includes reading what is not said in words but is made explicit in gestures or in silences that emerge and responding to those. In other words, being close to the other with all your attention, and at the same time resisting somewhat your urge to respond, opine, or judge what you are receiving. According to Sennett therein lies one of the most important keys for a good conversation, and for a true and enduring collaboration.

When listening, it is important that you choose what to focus on. Are you fully with the other or are you preoccupied with what your response is to her or his story? Are you already busy with formulating your answer? "Most people do not listen with the intent to understand; they listen with the intent to reply" is a famous quote by Stephen Covey (Covey, 1989).

Do you observe what the other is seeking to communicate and how this affects that person, but also what it does to you? In other words, do you feel where your own emotions surface, what touches you and what resonates with you? Sensing what the other is trying to say, how s/he experiences it and then finally distilling new meaning out of this together, requires listening with this kind of attention. So it is much more than only analytically listening to the content of what the other is saying. Being able to take in the content and the process has an important effect, discovered Harry van de Pol in a study of forty managers and their staff (Van de Pol, 2011). With a generative dialogue, it might not be about listening as a technical skill, but rather about listening attentively as a fundamental attitude, trying your best to be there fully, with whatever happens in the other, around you and within you, listening as if you have never been in that space before (Scharmer, 2009).

THE POWER OF ATTENTION

Listening requires attention; both for the other and for yourself. Managing your attention seems to have become an increasingly difficult and important quality or competency. Both in and outside organizations there is an increasing popularity of mindfulness courses and also theories in which *presence* plays an important role, such as in the work of Peter Senge et al (2004) and Otto Scharmer (2009). This could be due to the fact that there have never been so many possible distractions which eat away at our focus and there has never been so much information flowing toward us – just think of the streams of messages from all sorts of apps on our smartphones and mails.

In an essay on attention, Dutch social scientist, Andries Baart (2011) explores the different meanings of this concept, firstly, by focusing on its significance in the Dutch language. Remarkably there is no verb for attention, as there are for words such as memory, interest, thought and meaning. "I attention" or "you attention" does not exist in Dutch language, nor in English for that matter. Attention is always used together with a verb. We can *have* attention, *give* attention, *pay* attention, but also *ask, get, receive and beg for* attention and even *lose* attention. In the context of applying AI, we are mainly concerned with *directing* attention. Because "where and how we direct our attention is the key to what we create" says Otto Scharmer (2009).

In this context we can distinguish between two types of attention:

- Focused attention. This form of attention is selective and strongly directed. It is mainly known as *concentration*. When we talk of attention, concentrating usually comes to mind. For instance a manager, knowing precisely what is demanded of him in order to finish the annual plan, directs all of his attention to completing this task. He requests input from his staff and locks himself up for a few hours so that he can focus all his attention on writing the plan. This type of attention keeps other extrinsic signals at bay and has an isolating or excluding feature. The great thing with this kind of attention is that you can really achieve things, make significant progress or carry out very complex duties or tasks. At the same time, there are also disadvantages and risks attached, such that you can be totally oblivious of other important signals from the outside world. You might risk missing useful distractions.

- Unfocused attention. This type of attention lacks a specific focus or direction. It is more a state of alertness or vigilance, being receptive to what happens. For example, a manager walking around the work floor and making small talk with colleagues or in the context of a meeting, leaving space to discuss current affairs or issues in addition to the issues that were on the agenda. We call this *working with what is present*. Even though your attention is not focused on a prior selected topic, it can get hooked on something. For instance, on that colleague with whom you enter into conversation and who turns out to be dealing with an urgent problem at home or on a topic that generates a lot of energy and takes a full hour of talking during a meeting. The risk is that your attention gets hooked on that one specific subject, where other topics may be just as urgent but remain uncovered. Unfocused attention is more difficult to capture than focused attention and, according to Baart, is also less methodological. The quality of unfocused attention is closely associated with the *person* who has that attention.

You need both types of attention to a certain measure. There can be too much attention, or as Andries Baart suggests, "Attention is peaceful – but that does not mean to say that the excessive form (…) does not exist: obtrusive attention" (Baart, 2011).

BEING AWARE OF YOUR ATTENTION

Applying Appreciative Inquiry to encourage positive change calls for you to be aware of your attention and what you focus on. This applies both to the focused and the unfocused attention, and also to attention for you and for the other. But what does this mean in daily practice? What could Roald, the manager in our first example do in his daily life if he wants to be more attentive in his work?

In our practice, we see managers experimenting with the following tangible activities:

- Varying between focused and unfocused attention; making an assessment of your working week and deciding what form of attention might be appropriate given the schedule ahead. Do the forms of attention match with what you are seeking to achieve? Is there space to experiment by alternating between both types of attention?

- Making space for unfocused attention. Do you experience enough space for unfocused attention and do you know how you can make room for this? For example, by liberating a few hours a week in your schedule or by scheduling coffee machine talks when there is some slack, by switching your smartphone off, walking around, by reflecting in your car, engaging in a sport, practicing yoga, walking, or doing nothing. Managers identify these moments as important periods of unfocused attention that they would not want to miss out on.

- Keeping up your attention during the conversation. There are ways to keep your attention focused on the other. For instance, by regularly summarizing what the other is saying, by taking notes or by asking probing questions. The questions in a protocol for an AI-interview are an effective support for this. You can challenge yourself by actively reading between the lines. How is somebody seated? What does her voice sound like? What emotion does the other show? Articulating the emotions in the form of a reflection – I see that this affects you, it makes you angry, it makes you enthusiastic – enables you to check if your reading of emotions is accurate, and to include this in the conversation.

There is no standard recipe for attention; four hours of weekly attention for subject X or a weekly hour of attention for staff member Y. Finding the appropriate measure of attention that suits your organization or that moment in time, already calls for attention in and of itself.

INTERVIEW: ROLAND DE WOLF – PUNCH POWERTRAIN

IF YOU WANT TO CREATE COMMITMENT, WORKING IN A BOTTOM-UP MANNER IS THE ONLY WAY.

Roland De Wolf is operations manager with Punch Powertrain in Sint-Truiden. Punch is a company in the automotive sector that develops and produces drive systems and is currently one of the top companies in its sector. Based on his role and responsibility, Roland is the driving force of an internal initiative that aims at self-management and quality of collaboration in teams. This initiative is called CRT – continuously responsible teams.

PEOPLE MAKE THE MOVEMENT

I think that we went through quite a remarkable organizational development in recent years. What makes me most happy is seeing that our people are really in motion, even more, they are the ones who make the movement. One of the key factors in our development was our project on employee engagement called, *Coming to work with a smile on your face.* We faced considerable challenges in our factory, and we felt that committed staff members would form the key to success. Committed to me implies that everyone wants to do their best and is prepared to go to the finish line, and that management works from a strong confidence in our staff. Those two things go hand in hand and were the focus of the project- explicit support from top management and working from the bottom-up.

TAKING THE FIRST STEP

The most challenging thing for me was that we did not have a plan. Whenever we acquire a new machine, or adopt a new marketing strategy, we make a plan. But with a topic such as engagement and commitment, that is not possible. We really had to approach it in a different way. Therefore, we first invested in common understanding. In my case, the first step was an in-depth conversation on commitment with the team that reported directly to me. I discovered that everyone had the same ambition and voiced the same desire, albeit in different words.

215

LEARNING BY DOING

After this initial conversation, we expanded the group and repeated the conversation with more people, and so on. We investigated what commitment meant and what was needed to increase it. And we experimented with new ideas that came from these conversations. At times we even took a step backward. When I look back, we approached this project as a continuous learning and discovery process. Perhaps out of necessity, as it was all new to us. We could not fall back on routines and we discovered that there is no recipe for these types of questions. So, we invented our route along the way.

One of the principles that we adopted was to focus our energy on those colleagues who wanted to move forward and participate. Gradually we saw this group expand, largely because people heard from other colleagues that they were *really* being listened to, and that attention was paid to themes that were relevant to them. Those that hesitated or even were resistant eventually faced a choice: Do I join or do I remain behind?

SEEING EACH OTHER

When I look at our process as an illustration of Appreciative Inquiry, it all centers on the realization that in an organization people need to see each other. I mean seeing each other as human beings. What does someone feel, think? What is he good at? What does he need? In our company, the people on the work floor are the ones who are actually doing the job; they are the most important. It is them who we need to support and ensure that they are feeling good, as at the end of the day they generate our output. That is the reason why our organizational structure is a reversed pyramid, operators are at the top and the rest of the employees and managers support them.

A GREAT COMPANY

Meanwhile, we are seeing great results from all this work. The Board looks at our operations with confidence. When visitors come by, they tell us that the atmosphere in our company is great and that our story is inspirational. When asked, our employees state that personal attention for their wellbeing and opinion is the most important feature of Power Punch's organizational culture. New colleagues tell us, "What I see here, I have never seen in a company before!"

The best compliment I get is when colleagues have visited other companies and they come back and say that we can be proud of ourselves.

MOMENTS OF DOUBT

Were there moments of doubt? Yes, of course. After we completed our trajectory on commitment, we wanted to work on self-management by starting with the concept of CRT: *continuously responsible teams.* There was some hesitation, as once again we were unsure where and how to start. I stood up and said: "We will do this, and I will take full responsibility." I did not want to wait until everyone was ready, and we selected a first team that we thought would do well. We did that deliberately, so that we would soon have a first example to inspire others. But when you start something difficult and it fails, then everything falls apart, so it was challenging, but it went well.

We always kept giving attention to employees and kept putting that first, even in times when the company struggled. It is actually then that we had to persevere, as otherwise the project would have collapsed. We never asked for a plan, nor did we make one. Finding out what works and building on that was our working principle. Seeing something evolve provides enough confidence to continue. Continuously asking the question: What is going well and how can we use that to proceed? This has been another conscious choice in the entire process. Letting go and not knowing everything, is something that I needed to learn. It helped that I had a new direction to hold on to, namely to be appreciative. When I am appreciative, I can inspire and be infectious.

READY FOR THE FUTURE

The whole project gives us confidence for the future. We are facing an important period, as we foresee a strong growth for the company. Preparing for this growth, we have developed a new structure based on continuously responsible teams. We achieved this with the managers who are directly involved. We never decided for them but did it all together. Besides, not only the structure will change, their role is also affected. I believe that we are now prepared for any future growth which will bring the real potential of the teams to the fore.

EPILOGUE: CONTINUE SEARCHING TOGETHER

By Professor Emeritus René Bouwen

This practice-focused book is a call to managers and directors to seek concrete and achievable expressions of their responsibility as change process facilitators. Being present appreciatively with employees, in speaking and in acting, in the here and now, instantly offers clues that can be used to fuel change and development. The message of this book – which I would summarize as: search together for what works – may appear easy, and possibly quite obvious. It is in line with basic common sense of people who have positive intentions with and for each other. But it calls for authenticity and especially for mutual commitment that is so easily swept aside in our world of professionalization of organizational life, ruled by scientific research. Appreciative Inquiry makes this seemingly common-sense approach come alive and helps us experience directly how this approach can be realized. The underlying appreciative philosophy is rooted in relational social theory and a method of action research that provides a scientific foundation.

The authors have drawn on their extensive experience in a range of different organizational settings and on their contacts in an international network of professionals and researchers who apply Appreciative Inquiry in a great diversity of profit and social-profit organizations. In this epilogue we would like to focus for a moment on the uniqueness of this appreciative approach and situate this perspective within the very demanding, complex and fragmented current organizational context.

A RELATIONAL INTERPRETATION OF EXPERTISE

The appreciative approach is based on a knowledge and competency perspective that is grounded in a participatory practice of joint searching in projects and working groups. Knowledge is not located between the ears of people, but rather between the noses or in the interaction with each other. Of course, you need people's brains at work. The difference, however, is made by the quality of the interplay and the quality of the joint cooperation on projects in shared ownership. In this sense, expertise, and the application of expertise, acquires a different meaning.

In a scientific world we generally view expertise as the exceptional contribution of an expert who, often removed and from a distance, provides objective input. Such a view of expertise, which can be effective for strictly technical problem-solving, is just one component of the expertise that can change or improve a social system. Working collectively in an organization is an expertise which, at its core, is the result of the interplay of all the actors involved; an expertise born from experiential learning in the social system. The actors work and learn together and an expert or a manager can assist by orchestrating or facilitating but can definitely not apply expertise from the outside.

The appreciative approach takes an angle that makes this shared searching and aligning alive and powerful. The specificity consists of setting life-giving powers in motion by a process of joint inquiry and by making the quality of the interaction truly reciprocal. A dancing pair or a singing duo is possibly a good metaphor for such a high-quality practice. Jointly they work on a well-defined task and at the same time there is a personal relationship that is open, continuously reciprocal, consistently verifiable and challengeable. When a concrete result is achieved, a strong connection is realized that also leads to continuous learning.

A NEW INTERPLAY BETWEEN MANAGER AND EMPLOYEE

Managers may discover and develop the slumbering social expertise in their organization in interplay with employees by asking the right searching questions. Consultants or internal experts can help to create the necessary conditions to realize this teamwork, but eventually, managers and their staff are the designers and builders of change processes in organizations. Therefore, it is of value that this book is aimed directly at managers, exploring that essentially social-creative part of their organizational role: the ongoing joint searching for what the possibilities are here and now.

CONVERSING IS ALSO ABOUT DOING

A quality that needs to be emphasized is that dialogue, as the process of joint conversation and searching, is not only about verbal interaction but just as much about collaborative doing and collaborative working. A large share of any manager's time is spent on talking about, but it is the talking with each other and, even more so, the joint doing that ensures that connections are formed. In sports teams, this action component is very visible; providing an assist pass in soccer is equally as important as scoring a goal. Craftsmen can still experience this collaborative working together first hand. In the manufacturing industry, however, much of the group work has been replaced by compartmentalized, cognitive and digitalized tasks. As a result, the experience of establishing close connections in working with each other is less obvious. Hence, questions have become important as a connective element, helping us to overcome demarcation lines or boundaries. The appreciative inquiry approach (re)confirms and (re)connects people in their daily actions enabling them to see and realize new opportunities for the future.

BEYOND A FOCUS ON THE INDIVIDUAL

This joint searching transcends the strong individual orientation that currently reigns in so many organizations. There is a general tendency to subscribe both success and failure to individual achievements and responsibilities. However, our social system is increasingly shaped through the wider economic, social and political context which is strongly international. So, connecting people and jointly looking for new approaches and solutions is ever more important. The appreciative approach aims to strengthen the relational processes amongst actors in teams, project groups, business units, supply chains, networks at all sublevels – to align and unify the social system of organizations and institutions. Progress and development in almost every topic or domain of work is carried forward by such generative relational connections between all actors, and by embedding such connections in vital work relationships. The authors share an abundance of examples of such dialogical and relational practices in small groups and larger organizational settings.

In scientific literature, the underlying social-relational theory of AI is referred to as social constructionism – initially outlined by Professor Kenneth Gergen and a growing group of social-psychologists. In this paradigm, the social world is not regarded as a determined given reality that needs to be discovered in measurable terms. Rather the social reality is permanently in progress, while we are talking and searching with each other. Inquiry is the process of continuously co-constructing that what is being discovered and created. In his book *Relational Being, Beyond Self and Community* Kenneth Gergen (2009) poses the importance of relations at the core in the development of both the individual and the community. It is not the individual person, but the quality of the interplay that is regarded as the primary building block of social systems. Communities are not carried by structures or rules. Rather, these can only function if they germinate from powerful relational connections.

GENERATIVE, RATHER THAN POSITIVE

The appreciative approach has attracted a lot of attention in recent years. Maybe because working with the positive, supported by the growing field of positive psychology, leads to enthusiasm among many. Focusing on the positive side of things however nearly automatically calls out the negative counter point or shadow-side. It is important to emphasize recent developments that transcend the question about positivity or negativity. The question then becomes: What practices are most likely to lead to generative connections? What focus or question generates openness to the future *and* establishes the connections between parties that are necessary to continue working with each other in a sustainable manner? Generativity has a new and central significance in AI work; it is perhaps an even more apt term for the approaches described in this book than the words appreciate or appreciative.

APPRECIATIVE INQUIRY AS A DAILY PRACTICE

Embracing the AI approach is inevitably a social learning approach which is based on doing things together. An experienced facilitator can assist in getting things going and may help to set up the initial working methods. But the insights, attitudes and competencies of the joint searching may become part of the organizational culture. The daily work methods – dividing tasks and following through, making decisions, initiating and implementing projects, client contacts and collaboration with external parties – can be informed, honed, and elaborated according to appreciative principles.

Maybe, most important, is that people can experience the mildness and the energy of the appreciative attitude as an underlying philosophy of life; a way of being, not only doing. Especially in the daily interaction between employees, appreciative practices can find their way in as the basic attitude from which to approach things. The appreciative philosophy can be a deepening and enriching influence in everyone's personal life beyond work. Keeping a permanent eye out on possibilities, and always searching together for what works, here and now, can help us to thrive and flourish in our daily work and life.

REFERENCES

Amabile, T., & Kramer, S. (2012). *The progress principle: The progress principle: using small wins to ignite joy, engagement, and creativity at work.* Harvard Business Review Press.

Aragon, L. *Le fou d'Elsa.* Editions Gallimard.

Baart, A. (2014). *Aandacht: Etudes in presentie.* Boom Lemma Uitgevers.

Barrett, F. (2012). *Yes to the mess: Surprising leadership lessons from jazz.* Harvard Business Review Press.

Barrett, F., Fry, R. (2005). *Appreciative inquiry: A positive approach to building cooperative capacity.* Taos Institute Publications.

Beck, J. (2010). *The ecology of conversation: learning to communicate from your core.* Trafford Publishing.

Bouwen, G., & Meeus, M. (2011). *Vuur werkt: met talent toekomst maken.* LannooCampus.

Bronson, P. (2007). How Not to Talk to Your Kids: The inverse power of praise. In: *New York Magazine,* 3 August 2007.

Brown, T. (2009). *Change by design. How design thinking transforms organizations and inspires innovation.* HarperCollins Publishers.

Brown, J., & Isaacs, D. (2005). *The world café: Shaping our futures through conversations that matter.* Berrett-Koehler Publishers.

Buckingham, M. (2007). *Go put your strengths to work: 6 powerful steps to achieve outstanding performance.* Free Press.

Buckingham, M., & Clifton, D.O. (2001). *Now, discover your strengths.* Simon and Schuster.

Bunker, B.B., & Alban, B.T. (1997). *Large group interventions: Engaging the whole system for rapid change.* Jossey-Bass.

Bushe, G.R., & Kassam, A.F. (2005). When is appreciative inquiry transformational? A meta-case analysis. In: *The Journal of Applied Behavioral Science, 41*(2), 161-181.

Bushe, G. (2007). Appreciative inquiry is not about the positive. In: *OD practitioner, 39*(4), 33-38.

Bushe, G.R. (2011). Appreciative inquiry: Theory and critique. In: *The Routledge companion to organizational change*, 87-103.

Bushe, G.R. (2013). Generative process, generative outcome: The transformational potential of appreciative inquiry. In D.L. Cooperrider, D.P. Zandee, L.N. Godwin, M. Avital & B. Boland (eds.). *Organizational Generativity: The Appreciative Inquiry Summit and a Scholarship of Transformation (Advances in Appreciative Inquiry, Volume 4)*, Emerald Group Publishing Limited, pp. 89□ 113.

Bushe, G.R., & Marshak, R.J. (2014). Dialogic organization development. In B.B. Jones & M. Brazzel (eds.). *The NTL handbook of organization development and change*, Pfeiffer, pp. 193-211.

Caluwé, L.D., & Vermaak, H. (2006). *Leren veranderen. Een handboek voor de veranderkundige*. Kluwer.

Cameron, K.S., & Spreitzer, G.M. (eds.). (2011). *The Oxford handbook of positive organizational scholarship*. Oxford University Press.

Casserley & Megginson (2008). *Developing sustainable leaders and avoiding career derailment*. Elsevier/Butterworth-Heinemann.

Collins, J.C., & Porras, J.I. (2005). *Built to last: Successful habits of visionary companies*. Random House.

Cooperrider, D.L. (1986). *Appreciative Inquiry: Toward a methodology for understanding and enhancing organizational innovation*. Unpublished Ph.D., Case Western Reserve University, Cleveland.

Cooperrider, D.L., & Srivastva, S. (1987). Appreciative inquiry in organizational life. In: W.A. Pasmore & R.W. Woodman (eds.), *Research in Organizational Change and Development, Vol. 1, pp. 129-169*. JAI Press.

Cooperrider, D.L. (1999). Positive Image, Positive Action: The Affirmative Basis of Organizing. In: Srivastva, S. and Cooperrider, D. *Appreciative Management and Leadership*. Lakeshore Communications: 91-125.

Cooperrider, D.L., Whitney, D.K., & Stavros, J.M. (2003). *Appreciative inquiry handbook* (Vol. 1). Berrett-Koehler Publishers.

Cooperrider, D., & Whitney, D.D. (2005). *Appreciative inquiry: A positive revolution in change*. Berrett-Koehler Publishers.

Covey, S.R. (1989). *The 7 Habits of Highly Effective People: Powerful Lessons in Personal Change*. Free Press.

Dewulf, L., & Verheijen, L. (2004). Appreciative Inquiry: hoe onderzoeken en veranderen samen kunnen vallen. Een interview met David Cooperrider. In: *Opleiding & Ontwikkeling, 17* (11), 23-26.

Dewulf, L. (2009). *Ik kies voor mijn talent.* Scriptum.

Dutton, J.E. (2014). Build High-Quality Connections. In: Dutton, J. & G. M. Spreitzer (eds.) (2014). *How to be a positive leader: small actions, big impact.* Berrett-Koehler Publishers

Dweck, C. (2007). *Mindset: The New Psychology of Success.* Ballantine Books.

Frederickson, B. & Losada, M.F. (2005). Positive Affect and the Complex Dynamics of Human Flourishing. *American Psychologist, 60*(7), 678-686.

Fredrickson, B. (2009) *Positivity: Ground-Breaking Research Reveals How to Embrace the Hidden Strength of Positive Emotions, Overcome Negativity and Thrive.* Random House.

Gergen, K.J. (2009). *Relational being: Beyond self and community.* Oxford University Press.

Golden-Biddle, K. (2014) Create micro-moves for organizational change. In: Dutton, J. & G. M. Spreitzer (eds.) (2014). *How to be a positive leader: small actions, big impact.* Berrett-Koehler Publishers.

Groysberg, B. & Slind, J. (2012). *Talk, Inc.: How Trusted Leaders Use Conversation to Power Their Organizations.* Harvard Business Review Press.

Homan, T.H. (2008). *De binnenkant van organisatieverandering.* Kluwer.

Kabalt, J. (2012). *Curacao, our Nation. An Appreciative Inquiry about the future of Curacao.* Conference Paper for the World Appreciative Inquiry Conference 2012, Gent.

Kabalt, J. (2014). Experimenteren met Pleinen. In: *Opleiding & Ontwikkeling,* nr 3, p.18-24.

Kahane, A. (2010). *Power and love: A theory and practice of social change.* Berrett-Koehler Publishers.

Kessels, J.W.M. (2012). Leiderschapspraktijken in een professionele ruimte. Oratie. Heerlen: Open Universiteit.

Kotter, J.P. (1996). *Leading change.* Harvard Business Press.

Kotter, J.P. (2007). Leading change: Why transformation efforts fail. In: *IEEE Engineering Management Review,* vol 37, no. 3.

Koenen, E. (2011). *De kunst van leiderschap in tijden van verandering.* Boom/ Nelissen.

Koestenbaum, P. (2002). *Leadership, New and Revised: The Inner Side of Greatness, A Philosophy for Leaders.* John Wiley & Sons.

Lewin, K. (1951). *Field theory in social science: selected theoretical papers.* Harper & Brothers.

Ludema, J.D., Cooperrider, D.L., & Barrett, F.J. (2006). Appreciative inquiry: The power of the unconditional positive question. In: Reason, P. & H. Bradbury (eds.). *Handbook of action research: The concise paperback edition*, pp. 155-165. Sage.

Marquardt, M.J. (2011). *Leading with questions: How leaders find the right solutions by knowing what to ask.* John Wiley & Sons.

Masselink, R., van den Nieuwenhof, R. & De Jong, J. e.a. (2008). *Waarderend Organiseren: Appreciative Inquiry, co-creatie van duurzame verandering.* Gelling Publishing.

Masselink, R. & IJbema, J. (2011). *Het waarderend werkboek: Appreciative Inquiry in de praktijk.* Gelling Publishing.

Mau, B., & Leonard, J. (2004). *Massive change.* Phaidon.

Mohr, B.J., & Watkins, J.M. (2001). *Resource book for appreciative inquiry: A constructive approach to organizational development.* NTL Institute.

Nonaka, I., & Takeuchi, H. (1995). *The knowledge-creating company: How Japanese companies create the dynamics of innovation.* Oxford University Press.

Oldenburg, R. (1998). *The great good place: Cafes, coffee shops, bookstores, bars, hair salons, and other hangouts at the heart of a community.* Da Capo Press.

Orem, S., Binkert, J., & Clancy, A. (2007). *Appreciative Coaching: A Positive Process for Change.* Wiley.

Pollak, K. (2008). *Leren van de mensen in je leven: voor betere communicatie in het dagelijks leven.* Lev.

Pol, H. van de (2011). Luisteren is geen soft skill. In: *Management Scope*, nr. 6/7, p. 50-51.

Quinn, R. E. (2004) *Building the Bridge as You Walk on It: A Guide for Leading Change.* Jossey Bass.

Polanyi, M. (1966). *The Tacit Dimension.* Doubleday and Co

Rosen, S. (Ed.) (2010). *My voice will go with you: the teaching tales of Milton H. Erickson.* Norton.

Rotmans, J. (2014). *Verandering van tijdperk. Nederland kantelt.* Aeneas, Uitgeverij voor Vakinformatie.

Rusbridger, A. (2006). *Life is beautiful.* https://www.theguardian.com/music/2006/dec/13/classicalmusican-dopera.secondworldwar

Scharmer, C.O. (2009). *Theory U: Learning from the future as it emerges.* Berrett-Koehler Publishers.

Senge, P.M. (1990). *The fifth discipline: The art and practice of the learning organization.* Currency Doubleday.

Sennett, R. (2012). *Together: The rituals, pleasures and politics of cooperation.* Yale University Press.

Shaw, P. (2002). *Changing conversations in organizations: A complexity approach to change.* Psychology Press.

Smid, G.A.C. et al (2006). Learning histories in leer- en veranderingstrajecten. Geschiedenis maken vanuit hart voor de zaak. In: Boonstra, J. & L. de Caluwé (eds.). *Interveniëren en veranderen. Zoeken naar betekenis in interacties.* Kluwer.

Smit, C. & Tjepkema, S. (2001): *Alles wat je aandacht geeft, groeit.* Reed.

Smit, C., P. Pillen & S. Tjepkema (2010). Echt ander gedrag in 40 dagen. In: Lazeron, N. & R. van Dinteren (red.). *Brein@Work.* Bohn Stafleu van Loghem.

Snowden, D.J., & Boone, M.E. (2007). A leader's framework for decision making. In: *Harvard Business Review, 85* (11), 68.

Stacey, R.D. (1996). *Complexity and creativity in organizations.* Berrett-Koehler Publishers.

Stacey, R. (2001) *Complex Responsive Processes in Organizations.* Routledge.

Stacey, R.D. (2010). *Complexity and organizational reality. Uncertainty and the need to rethink management after the collapse of investment capitalism.* Routledge.

Stone Zander, R., & Zander, B. (2002). *The art of possibility: Transforming professional and personal life.* Penguin.

Streatfield, P.J. (2001). *The paradox of control in organizations.* Psychology Press.

Swart, C. (2013). *Re-authoring the world: the narrative lens and practices for organisations, communities and individuals.* Knowledge Resources.

Swieringa, J. & A. Wierdsma (1992). *Op weg naar een lerende organisatie.* Wolters-Noordhoff.

Thatchenkerry, T. & Metzker, C. (2006). *Appreciative Intelligence: seeing the mighty oak in the acorn.* Berrett-Koehler Publishers.

Tesselaar, S. & A. Scheringa (2009). *Storytelling handboek: organisatieverhalen voor managers, trainers en onderzoekers.* Boom.

Tjepkema, S. (2010). Leren door proberen: experimenten in het werk. In: Gijbels, D. & Raemdonck, I. van (red.), *Develop: leerpotentieel van de werkplek.* No. 3, pp. 35-41. Springer.

Tjepkema, S. & M. van Rooij (2010). Grumpy moments…. In: *Opleiding & Ontwikkeling,* jrg. 23, nr. 5, p. 60.

Tjepkema, S. & Verheijen, L. (2009). *Van kiem tot kracht: Een waarderend perspectief voor persoonlijke ontwikkeling en organisatieverandering.* Springer.

Tjepkema, S. & Verheijen, L. (2012). Appreciative Inquiry. In: Ruijters, M. & Simons, R.J. (red.). *Canon van het leren. 50 concepten en hun grondleggers* (pp. 77-89). Kluwer.

Tjepkema, S. & Kabalt, J. (2012). Appreciative Inquiry: veranderen met energie. Kessels & Smit publicatie.

Ueland, B. (1998). *Tell me more.* Kore Press.

Van den berg, B, van der Harst, A., Fortuin-van der Spek, C & Wassink, H. (2011) *Onze school is een verhaal.* CPS.

Verdonschot, S. (2014). Het geheim van de smid: nieuwsgierigheid. In: *Opleiding & Ontwikkeling,* jrg. 27, nr. 3, pp. 55-56.

Verdonschot, S. & Spruyt, M. (2015). *Nieuwsgierigheid op het werk.* Kessels & Smit Publishers.

Vogt, E.E., Brown, J., & Isaacs, D. (2003). *The Art of Powerful Questions: Catalyzing, Insight, Innovation, and Action.* Whole Systems Associates.

Wanrooij, M. (2004). Coachen van professionals: sturen op resultaten en ontwikkeling. In: Kwakman, F. (red.) *Professionals en professionele ontwikkeling.* Academic Service.

Whitney, D., Cooperrider, D., Trosten-Bloom, A., & Kaplin, B.S. (2005). *Encyclopedia of positive questions. Volume One. Using Appreciative Inquiry to Bring Out the Best in Your Organization.* Crown Custom Publishing.

Whitney, D., Trosten-Bloom, A., & Rader, K. (2010). *Appreciative leadership: Focus on what works to drive winning performance and build a thriving organization.* McGraw Hill Professional.

Whitney, D., & Trosten-Bloom, A. (2010). *The power of appreciative inquiry: A practical guide to positive change.* Berrett-Koehler Publishers.

Whitney, D., A. Trosten-Bloom, J. Cherney & R. Fry (2004). *Appreciative team building: positive questions to bring out the best of your team.* iUniverse.

Zach, P. J. (2015) "Why Inspiring Stories Make Us React: The Neuroscience of Narrative." *Cerebrum*, Jan-Feb: 2

Zandee, D.P. (2013). The Process of Generative Inquiry. In D.L. Cooperrider, D.P. Zandee, L.N. Godwin, M. Avital & B. Boland (eds.). *Organizational Generativity: The Appreciative Inquiry Summit and a Scholarship of Transformation (Advances in Appreciative Inquiry, Volume 4),* Emerald Group Publishing Limited, pp. 69-88.

Taos Institute Publications

See all the Taos Publications at:
https://www.taosinstitute.net/taos-books-and-publications

Taos Institute Publications Books in Print

* * * * * * *

Taos Tempo Series:
Taos Tempo Series: Collaborative Practices for Changing Times

Thriving Women, Thriving World: An Invitation to Dialogue, Healing and Inspired Actions (2019) by Diana Whitney, Caroline Adams Miller, Tanya Cruz Teller, Marlene Ogawa, Jessica Cocciolone, Haesun Moon, Kathryn Britton, Angela Koh & Alejandra Leon de la Barra (also available as an e-book)

Paths to Positive Aging: Dog Days with a Bone and other Essays, (2017) by Kenneth J. Gergen and Mary Gergen

The Magic of Organizational Life, (2017) by Mette Larsen

70Candles! Women Thriving in their 8th Decade, (2015) by Jane Giddan and Ellen Cole (also available as an e-book)

Social Constructionist Perspectives on Group Work, (2015) by Emerson F. Rasera, editor.

U & Me: Communicating in Moments that Matter, (Revised edition 2014) by John Steward (also available as an e-book)

Relational Leading: Practices for Dialogically Based Collaborations, (2013) by Lone Hersted and Ken Gergen (also available as an e-book)

Retiring but Not Shy: Feminist Psychologists Create their Post-Careers, (2012) by Ellen Cole and Mary Gergen. (also available as an e-book)

Developing Relational Leadership: Resources for Developing Reflexive Organizational Practices, (2012) by Carsten Hornstrup, Jesper Loehr-Petersen, Joergen Gjengedal Madsen, Thomas Johansen, Allan Vinther Jensen (also available as an e-book)

Practicing Relational Ethics in Organizations, (2012) by Gitte Haslebo and Maja Loua Haslebo

Healing Conversations Now: Enhance Relationships with Elders and Dying Loved Ones, (2011) by Joan Chadbourne and Tony Silbert

Riding the Current: How to Deal with the Daily Deluge of Data, (2010) by Madelyn Blair

Ordinary Life Therapy: Experiences from a Collaborative Systemic Practice, (2009) by Carina Håkansson

Mapping Dialogue: Essential Tools for Social Change, (2008) by Marianne "Mille" Bojer, Heiko Roehl, Mariane Knuth-Hollesen, and Colleen Magner

Positive Family Dynamics: Appreciative Inquiry Questions to Bring Out the Best in Families, (2008) by Dawn Cooperrider Dole, Jen Hetzel Silbert, Ada Jo Mann, and Diana Whitney

* * * * * * *

Focus Book Series

STAN and The Four Fantastic Powers: The First Appreciative Inquiry Book for Kids, (2018) by Shira Levy, Marge Schiller, Sarah Schiller, Max Schiller, and illustrator, Stehanie Rudolph.

Coordinated Management of Meaning, CMM: A Research Manual, (2017) by Natalie Rascon and Stephen Littlejohn (also available as an e-book)

Communicating Possibilities: A Brief Introduction to the Coordinated Management of Meaning (CMM), (2017) by Ilene C. Wasserman and Beth Fisher-Yoshida (also available as an e-book)

A Student's Guide to Clinical Supervision, (2014) by Glenn E. Boyd

When Stories Clash: Addressing Conflict with Narrative Mediation, (2013) by Gerald Monk and John Winslade (also available as an e-book)

Bereavement Support Groups: Breathing Life Into Stories of the Dead (2012) by Lorraine Hedtke (also available as an e-book)

The Appreciative Organization, Revised Edition (2008) by Harlene Anderson, David Cooperrider, Ken Gergen, Mary Gergen, Sheila McNamee, Jane Watkins, and Diana Whitney

Appreciative Inquiry: A Positive Approach to Building Cooperative Capacity, (2005) by Frank Barrett and Ronald Fry (also available as an e-book)

Dynamic Relationships: Unleashing the Power of Appreciative Inquiry in Daily Living, (2005) by Jacqueline Stavros and Cheri B. Torres

Appreciative Sharing of Knowledge: Leveraging Knowledge Management for Strategic Change, (2004) by Tojo Thatchenkery

Social Construction: Entering the Dialogue, (2004) by Kenneth J. Gergen, and Mary Gergen (also available as an e-book)

Appreciative Leaders: In the Eye of the Beholder, (2001) edited by Marge Schiller, Bea Mah Holland, and Deanna Riley

Experience AI: A Practitioner's Guide to Integrating Appreciative Inquiry and Experiential Learning, (2001) by Miriam Ricketts and Jim Willis

* * * * * * *

Books for Professionals Series

Appreciative Inquiry as a Daily Leadership Practice: Realizing Change One Conversation at a Time (2020) by Luc Verheijen, Saskia Tjepkema, Joeri Kabalt

Social Constructionist Perspectives on Group Work, (2015) by Emerson F. Rasera, editor.

New Horizons in Buddhist Psychology: Relational Buddhism for Collaborative Practitioners, (2010) edited by Maurits G.T. Kwee

Positive Approaches to Peacebuilding: A Resource for Innovators, (2010) edited by Cynthia Sampson, Mohammed Abu-Nimer, Claudia Liebler, and Diana Whitney

Social Construction on the Edge: 'Withness'-Thinking & Embodiment, (2010) by John Shotter

Joined Imagination: Writing and Language in Therapy, (2009) by Peggy Penn

Celebrating the Other: A Dialogic Account of Human Nature, (reprint 2008) by Edward Sampson

Conversational Realities Revisited: Life, Language, Body and World, (2008) by John Shotter

Horizons in Buddhist Psychology: Practice, Research and Theory, (2006) edited by Maurits Kwee, Kenneth J. Gergen, and Fusako Koshikawa

Therapeutic Realities: Collaboration, Oppression and Relational Flow, (2005) by Kenneth J. Gergen

SocioDynamic Counselling: A Practical Guide to Meaning Making, (2004) by R. Vance Peavy

Experiential Exercises in Social Construction – A Fieldbook for Creating Change, (2004) by Robert Cottor, Alan Asher, Judith Levin, and Cindy Weiser

Dialogues About a New Psychology, (2004) by Jan Smedslund

* * * * * * *

WorldShare Books – Free PDF Download

Cultural Dialogue at Home - Austrian Hosts and Syrian Refugees: An Autoethnographic Narrative. (PDF version 2019) By Corina Ahlers

A Systemic Community: Collaborative Leadership, Redescription and Evolutionary Ways of Becoming, (PDF version 2019), by Jacob Storch

Social Texts and Context: Literature and Social Psychology, (PDF version 2018), by Jonathan Potter, Peter Stringer, Margaret Wetherell

Lifescaping Project: Action Research and Appreciative Inquiry in San Francisco Bay Area Schools, (PDF version 2017), edited by Rolla E. Lewis, Ardella Dailey, Greg Jennings, Peg Windelman

Disarmed Warriors: Narratives with Youth Ex-Combatants in Colombia, (PDF version 2017), by Victoria Lugo

Spirituality, Social Construction and Relational Processes: Essays and Reflections (PDF version 2016) edited by Duane Bidwell.

Therapy as a Hermeneutic and Constructionist Dialogue: Practices of freedom and of deco-construction in the relational, language and meaning games (PDF version 2016) by Gilberto Limon (Translated from Spanish)

Recovered Without Treatment: The Process of Abandoning Crystal Meth Use Without Professional Help (PDF version 2016) by Pavel Nepustil

Introduction to Group Dynamics: Social Construction Approach to Organizational Development and

Community Revitalization, (PDF version 2016), by Toshio Sugiman

Recursos psico-sociales para el post-conflicto" (Psico-social resources for post-conflict) (PDF version 2016), Edited by Angela Maria Estrada

Buddha As Therapist: Meditations (PDF version 2015), by G.T. Maurits Kwee

Diálogos para la transformación: experiencias en terapia y Otras intervenciones psicosociales en Iberoamérica – Volumen 1 and 2 (PDF version 2015), by Dora Fried Schnitman, Editora

Education as Social Construction: Contributions to Theory, Research and Practice (PDF version 2015) Editors: Thalia Dragonas, Kenneth J. Gergen, Sheila McNamee, Eleftheria Tseliou

Psychosocial Innovation in Post-War Sri Lanka (PDF version 2015) by Laurie Charles and Gameela Samarasinghe

Social Accountability & Selfhood (PDF version 2015, original publication date – 1984, Basil Blackwell, Inc.) by John Shotter

Construccionismo Social Y Discusion De Paradrigmas En Psycologia: Indeterminacion, Holismo y Juegos de Lenguaje vs. La Teoria Pictorica del Lenguaje (PDF versión 2015) by Roberto Aristequi

{In}Credible Leadership: A Guide for Shared Understanding and Application (PDF version 2015) by Yuzanne Mare, Isabel Meyer, Elonya Niehaus-Coetzee, Johann Roux

Etnia Terapéutica: Integrando Entornos (PDF version 2015) by Jeannette Samper A. and José Antonio Garciandía I.

Post-modern Education & Development (Chinese edition, PDF version 2014) Introduction by Shi-Jiuan Wu (後現代教育與發展　　介紹　吳熙琄)

Exceeding Expectations: An Anthology of Appreciative Inquiry Stories in Education from Around the World (PDF version 2014), Story Curators: Dawn Dole, Matthew Moehle, and Lindsey Godwin

The Discursive Turn in Social Psychology (PDF version 2014), by Nikos Bozatzis & Thalia Dragonas (Eds.)

New Paradigms, Culture and Subjectivity (PDF version 2014), Edited by Dora Fried Schnitman and Jorge Schnitman

Happily Different: Sustainable Educational Change – A Relational Approach (PDF version 2014), by Loek Schoenmakers

Strategising through Organising: The Significance of Relational Sensemaking, (PDF version 2013), by Mette Vinther Larsen

Therapists in Continuous Education: A Collaborative Approach, (PDF version 2013), by Ottar Ness

Contextualizing Care: Relational Engagement with/in Human Service Practices, (PDF version 2013), by Janet Newbury

Nuevos Paradigmas, Cultura y Subjetividad, by Dora Fried Schnitman

Novos Paradigmas Em Mediação, (PDF versión, original publicación date 1999). Dora Fried Schnitman y Stephen LittleJohn (editors)

Filo y Sofía En Diálogo: La poesía social de la conversación terapéutica, (PDF versión 2013, original publicación date 2000), Klaus G. Deissler y Sheila McNamee (editors). Traducción al español: Mario O. Castillo Rangel

Socially Constructing God: Evangelical Discourse on Gender and the Divine (PDF version 2013), by Landon P. Schnabel

Ohana and the Creation of a Therapeutic Community (PDF version 2013), by Celia Studart Quintas

From Nonsense Syllables to Holding Hands: Sixty Years as a Psychologist (PDF version 2013), by Jan Smedslund

Management and Organization: Relational Alternatives to Individualism (PDF version 2013), reprinted with permission. Edited by Dian Marie Hosking, H. Peter Dachler, Kenneth J. Gergen

Appreciative Inquiry to Promote Local Innovations among Farmers Adapting to Climate Change (PDF version 2013) by Shayamal Saha

La terapia Multi–Being. Una prospettiva relazionale in psicoterapia, (PDF versión 2013) by Diego Romaioli

Psychotherapy by Karma Transformation: Relational Buddhism and Rational Practice (PDF version 2013) by G.T. Maurits Kwee

La terapia como diálogo hermenéutico y construccionista: Márgenes de libertad y deco-construcción en los juegos relacionales, de lenguaje y de significado (PDF versión 2012) by Gilberto Limón Arce

Wittgenstein in Practice: His Philosophy of Beginnings, and Beginnings, and Beginnings (PDF version 2012) by John Shotter

Social Construction of the Person (PDF version 2012). Editors: Kenneth J. Gergen and Keith M. Davis, Original copyright date: 1985, Springer-Verlag, New York, Inc.

Images of Man (PDF version 2012) by John Shotter. Original copyright date: 1975, Methuen, London.

Ethical Ways of Being (PDF version 2012) by Dirk Kotze, Johan Myburg, Johann Roux, and Associates. Original copyright date: 2002, Ethics Alive, Institute for Telling Development, Pretoria, South Africa.

Piemp (PDF version 2012) by Theresa Hulme. Published in Afrikaans.

For book information and ordering, visit Taos Institute Publications at:
www.taosinstitutepublications.net

For further information, call: 1-888-999-TAOS, 1-440-338-6733
Email: info@taosoinstitute.net